D1433362

MOSTLY JOY
A Bookman's Story

Also by Thomas Joy

THE RIGHT WAY TO RUN A LIBRARY BUSINESS

BOOKSELLING

THE TRUTH ABOUT BOOKSELLING

The Author. Cartoon by Mickey Durling. (reproduced by kind permission of *Smith's Trade News*)

Mostly Joy

A BOOKMAN'S STORY

Thomas Joy

'And e'en while fashion's brightest arts decoy
The Heart distrusting asks, if this be joy.'
'The Deserted Village'—OLIVER GOLDSMITH

LONDON

MICHAEL JOSEPH

First published in Great Britain by
MICHAEL JOSEPH LTD
52 Bedford Square
London WC1
1971

© *1971 by Thomas Joy*

7181 0883 3

Printed in Great Britain by Northumberland Press Ltd.,
Gateshead, and bound by the Dorstel Press, Harlow

This book is dedicated to
Marjory and Ian Chapman

ACKNOWLEDGEMENTS

To Mrs Ivy Hobday who read the typescript and made very many valuable editorial suggestions, to Miss Mabel Riley who has typed all my books, and to Mrs Vera Goodman.

Finally to Eric Hiscock (Whitefriar) who after having read part of the manuscript encouraged me to finish it, and above all to my wife who helped with the book but more importantly is patient with me during the course of writing when I am unapproachable.

CONTENTS

LIST OF ILLUSTRATIONS

9

FOREWORD by DENNIS WHEATLEY

Memoirs are of two kinds. The vast majority are accounts of the lives of statesmen, generals and other great public figures, recounting their triumphs and either ignoring or glossing over their mistakes. A small minority—for example, those concerning such diverse figures as Pepys, Dr Johnson and Casanova—portray not only the person but also the age in which he lived. The latter are of infinitely more value to posterity, and Thomas Joy's book is one of them.

Tommy, whose youth was spent in Oxford, was a town-bred boy but had the countryside and the river close to his home; and he loved both. In his pages we see that famous city as it was when still the world's greatest seat of learning; not as it is now, its centuries' old character submerged in the industrial ratrace.

It is said that fortune favours the brave. It favours even more youngsters who throw their heart into their jobs, who see the best side in everyone they meet, and have the gift of ready laughter. Tommy's first labours at the Bodleian and in Oxford bookshops were not work to him, but fascinating opportunities to acquire knowledge and make friends. At the same time he enjoyed himself immensely, playing jokes, going to fairs, falling in the river and carousing with his contemporaries in age-old English pubs.

His career was meteoric. To London, buying up Mudies Library for Harrods—a terrible gamble—and disposing of it at a fine profit, deputy managing director at the Army and Navy Stores and, finally, head of Hatchards, the most famous bookshop in the world.

Yet in all those years of tireless endeavour he found the time to serve his profession better than any other bookseller. For three decades he has been the key figure on innumerable trade committees and charities, helped countless authors with their problems, initiated better conditions for staffs and devised original methods of salesmanship.

No request seems too small for him. Recently my wife wanted some children's paperbacks, but could not find those particular titles. To my horror I learned that she had rung up Tommy Joy. Those few shillings-worth of books were delivered next day.

When I first met him it was, I thought, as an enemy. In the 1930s 7s. 6d. was the normal price for a new novel. My publisher, Walter Hutchinson, decided to put his up to 8s. 6d. The four great subscription libraries were Boots, Smith, Harrods and the Times. If the rise became universal they would be forced to increase subscriptions.

As I was already a best-seller Hutchinson decided to use my new books as a guinea-pig, with the idea that the libraries would be forced to buy it. The four got together and decided to fight by cutting their orders for my book by 50%. Freddy Richardson of Boots, Mr Baker of W. H. Smith and Andrew Shirley of the Times were all old friends of mine and said they would do what they could for me by coming to some arrangement with Hutchinson; but they must all stick together. Tommy Joy had only just succeeded my good friend Cadness Page as chief librarian at Harrods. I had never met him, so went to see him. He proved adamant upon the issue; so I gained the impression that he was the nigger in the wood-pile. Intensely resenting my growing sales being crushed by a trade dispute between my publisher and the librarians, I took the stupid step of writing over Tommy's head to his chief, Sir Richard Burbidge. Naturally, he supported his librarian; so I got no change. A fortnight later a compromise was reached and the four librarians doubled their order for my book. But I felt that I had blotted my copy-book for good with Mr Joy, as he had every right to resent my having written to Sir Richard. I tell this story to show Tommy's generous nature. He saw my side of the picture, sympathised with my distress and did everything he could to push up my sales. From then on we have been the very best of friends.

The *double entendre* of the title of the book MOSTLY JOY has real meaning. In addition to much interesting information about the book trade, and the management of great London stores, there are scores of good laughs in it; amusing rhymes, near-bawdy songs and the fun of early flickering films.

Finally, as during his long career, and at his famous 'Authors of the Year' parties, Tommy must have met every British author of repute, and many so far more distinguished than myself, I must say how very flattered and honoured I am that he should have asked me to write this foreword.

MOSTLY JOY should prove the best autobiography of the year and, perhaps, for many years to come.

Dennis Wheatley

I

We would sit around the low brick wall which enclosed a big, chugging, brown-red boiler in the yard of the Co-operative Bakery in Henry Road, Oxford. It was warm there, and we could stir our melting jelly-babies on the boiler with a match-stick and eat them piping hot. As I recall it, the flavour was not at all improved but it was fun, and cooking anything has an attraction for children.

The boiler itself was by no means clean and many a child would pee on it, which too was fun, but one hopes the constant heat sterilised the cooking surface. To have jelly-babies to melt was a rare treat and although a good supply could be bought for a halfpenny, we did but rarely possess a halfpenny and few of my friends, as far as I knew, ever possessed more than a penny at a time. In those days children were lucky indeed if they received a penny a week pocket money, as the general attitude was the Victorian one that too much pocket money was bad for a child. But in my child-hood days one could go shopping for a few sweets for as little as a farthing. A Spanish Ribbon, which was a strip of licorice about a foot long, cost a halfpenny and two bull's-eyes another halfpenny.

We would tear gently down the thin ribs of the Spanish Ribbon to make it last longer, and the more generous of us would give a strip to a friend. Bull's-eyes were like giant marbles or Aggies* as we called them—and one's mouth was barely large enough to get one in and there was some danger of choking until, after prolonged sucking, it became as small as a cat's-eye, which was a sweet exactly the size of the usual marble. A Mrs Green had a very small shop in Hollybush Row where she sold her very special home-made toffee, eight pieces for a penny, but better still for a farthing we could buy a bag of 'chippings', just odd pieces broken in the process of manufacture. Delicious! and judged to be the best value for money. These were our favourite sweets together with everlasting strips—which was a strip of toffee, again about a foot long—sherbet dabs, aniseed balls and callybonkers, a toffee about the size of an ice cream wafer and very hard to bite.

Our pennies were so few and far between that we naturally wanted a lot for our money. We rarely bought chocolate because it went too quickly, but a small bar could be bought for a halfpenny, and a piece which now costs a shilling was a penny or at the most twopence.

Carlo, the ice-cream man, would come round the streets in the summer months with cornets at a halfpenny and wafers at a penny, but all too infrequently could we buy. I often think of this as I watch the best part of the young audience in a cinema today rush for ice-creams in the interval. Never has ice-cream tasted so good as the 'home-made' ice-cream made by those Italian vendors, Carlo and the Del Nevos, who first took it round the streets of Oxford.

In the winter the same men came round with a horse-drawn fish and chip cart, with a large pan of boiling oil above a coke fire. The tall chimney at the rear gave off a most appealing smell. One could buy a small bag of chips for a halfpenny and a large one for a penny. A piece of fried fish cost a penny and a really large piece twopence. We bought

* Aggies or Ally Marbles were large glass marbles usually with spirals of coloured glass in the centre. This was the one you tried to win when playing marbles or used like the jack in the game of bowls. Hence the expression, 'that's just my ally marble' meaning 'That's just what I would like'.

16

locusts*—a black bean about the size of a runner bean, perhaps not quite as long—from grocers and greengrocers. I never see them for sale in this country today, but I have seen them growing on trees in Portugal and in Majorca and in the South of France. They are used there for horse fodder. We ate them and I recall the outer skin was pretty tough and the inside was sweet, with little sugar crystals near the inside bean.

Another 'nut' we never see today is the 'tiger' nut.† It was, I suppose, some sort of ground-nut and to eat it was like chewing a small piece of sweet wood. As children we loved them and also pomegranates which one could eat slowly, seed by seed. Oranges were a luxury and, as I recall it, only available 'in season', which was about autumn and winter. Grapefruit were unknown. Glamorous film stars in the silent movies were often served breakfast in bed with grapefruit—for years I wondered what they were eating!

There were many children in Henry Road where we lived. It was a small street of about forty houses on one side—newly built around 1908—and, as the Bakery of the Co-operative Society took up much of the other side, only about twelve houses were there. I write in the past tense but the street is the same today. People had large families some fifty odd years ago. There was one family of thirteen in our street and several of from five to eight.

I was one of a family of seven, being the third to be born *and the only boy*. People imagine that the large families were due to there being few entertainments available to the poorer classes, together with a measure of drunkenness and lack of knowledge of preventive methods. All this, in some measure, is doubtless true, but a more important factor is, in my view, likely to be the operation of a law of nature which seems to bring about larger families when the death rate is

---

* The Carob or Locust bean from the Algorraba tree. It is called the locust because it is supposed to have been the food of John the Baptist in the wilderness (Matt. 3:4). It is also called St John's bread.
† Tiger nuts are the edible rhizome of Cyperus esculentus, a European sedge.

high. So many children died of the then common ailments—diphtheria, scarlet fever, pneumonia and tuberculosis—that unconsciously people were affected in their attitude to the size of families. There is historical evidence that during and after wars and plagues, people breed rapidly and the phenomenon is too common to be dismissed as just un-disciplined sex. Axel Munthe refers to this in his classic book, *The Story of San Michele.*

I never lived down my first childish mistakes—sisters have long memories. On one clear, starlit night, I looked at the stars and said to my mother, 'Look at the cinders.' When I wanted someone to open a door because I was too small to reach the handle, I said, 'Ope' or 'Opu'. My mother corrected me, 'O-pen,' she said. 'Think of a pen.' Next time I said, 'O-nib the door.' Well! anyone can make a mistake, as the hedgehog exclaimed as he jumped off the scrubbing-brush.

Henry Road was, as I have said, a street of fairly new houses and although life was doubtless hard at times for many, and money often scarce, the residents were, on the whole, comfortably off. Henry Road was quite a good address in West Oxford but North Oxford was regarded as *the* address until Boars Hill became fashionable, particularly for intellectuals. In those days as long as the man of the house was in regular work, the children were fed and clothed. A few in poorer areas in St Ebbes and St Thomas's had no shoes and some children could be seen with rickets due to under-nourishment, sometimes caused more by ignorance of correct diet than by lack of food.

We had the good fortune to be near the country, for Binsey Lane, with its fields and farms, was only a street or so away, and Hinksey Lane with the old ferry barge at Ferry Hinksey, leading to the seven cornfields, was also only a short walk from our home. The delightful Wytham fields were further away but still within walking distance.

The water tributaries of the Thames are a child's joy and there we picnicked with our bottles of water or lemonade made from a yellow powder which contained sugar, or cold tea—no thermos flasks in those days—and bread and butter with perhaps the heart of a home-grown lettuce, for all our fathers had gardens or allotments. Then maybe fish-paste sandwiches and a large hunk of home-made fruit cake would follow. Poorer families liked cold bread pudding.

Here in the water-meadows we saw the birds and found their nests—moorhens, plovers, finches, kingfishers, blackbirds, tits, wrens and thrushes. All the children I knew were familiar with the birds and could recognise their eggs and knew where to look for a particular nest; a swan's nest was viewed with awe from a distance. Here too, were flowers and grasses in profusion with kingcups (water buttercups) at the edge of the stream, bluebells in the woods and cowslips in the fields. Later in the year we picked quaking grass and ragged robins, and moon daisies in the lush meadows of standing grass before hay-making time. We caught tadpoles and sticklebacks in the smaller side streams and watched the magic of the moving 'sticks'—caddis-fly larvae, encased in wooden-like cocoons as long as a match-stick. There were frogs everywhere. Where have all the frogs gone? It is rare to see one in these same meadows today.

If our life was hard we did not know it. If we were, by today's standards, under-privileged, we did not realise it. We had the love of our parents and a happy family life. It was sufficient. One remembers being cold in the long winters —oh, how cold!—with numbed fingers. We pierced cocoa tins and filled them with old rags which smouldered when lit in the enclosed space and these warmed our fingers. We made small bonfires in the fields and roasted potatoes in them. We bowled hoops and played with tops. We were not cold at home as we had large coal fires and a kitchen range, but out at play in the streets and meadows and particularly at school, when the master would seal off the warmth from the one coal fire with his bottom. This injustice we accepted as we were brought up to respect our elders and all in authority. For a policeman to knock on any neighbour's door was just about the biggest disgrace a family could suffer; and if he called because of the misdemeanour of a child, it was the talk of the neighbourhood, and the parents would feel deeply the shame of it.

We had instilled into us something more than a healthy respect for the law and for authority generally. If we were caned at school we could expect no sympathy at home for doubtless 'you deserved it'. Not that our parents were hard but they kept their true feelings to themselves and had a common-sense psychology to apply, which was more beneficial than all this nonsense of today which makes children soft and too expectant.

Seeing my two older sisters going to school, I cried until my parents let me go too, and so I started school when I was three years old. I began at St Frideswides' Infant School and I can remember vividly my first day there with a Miss Bennett, schoolmistress. She was cross-eyed, which worried my mother as she was sure one could catch other people's mannerisms. 'Look at a fishmonger,' she would say. 'He has a face just like the fish on his slab.' It was always difficult to know just when Mother was serious or joking, and perhaps I got this idiosyncrasy from her, because my wife says the same thing about me. Mother had many amusing sayings: for example, 'It is like giving a donkey strawberries,' when something was wasted on someone, or, 'It runs in families like wooden legs,' when remarking on the peculiarities of someone. Sometimes these sayings were outstandingly ridiculous, as when of someone a bit simple, she would say, 'They would laugh to see a pudding crawl!'; sometimes profound as when an ungracious person behaved in an ill-bred way and she would say, 'What can one expect from a pig but a grunt?' Straight hair was 'as straight as a yard of pump water'.

We were blessed with remarkable parents. Of my father, Dean Rusk wrote to me from the White House following his death at the ripe age of eighty-nine, 'Your father was one of the kindest men I have ever known.' But it was Mother who was just an angel—she showed little of her affection for us and was absolutely undemonstrative but, as the years went by, I could see her love more clearly and knew more of the sacrifices she made. I realise now that we were her very life and she asked very little in return other than that we should be a credit to the family.

I was born in Isis Street just off Folly Bridge and the Thames ran at the bottom of our garden; and all my life I have been living on or near that river, which is my great good fortune. I love rivers but no river to me has the variety and charm of the Thames. One grows to love it from source to mouth and from dusk to dawn. It is ever changing but ever the same.

I swam, played in the water and in my youth took my girl-friends in a punt on the River Cherwell, which branches off from the Isis. The river means much to all the young and many not so young at Oxford. On May Day we would rise early to be at Magdalen Tower to see and hear the choristers singing from the top of the tower at sunrise. Afterwards we would watch the Morris dancers with their jingling bells worn below the knee and then take a boat on the Cherwell or cycle off to the water-meadows to pick snakesheads (fritillaries) which grew wild in the water-meadows at Iffley—one of the very few places in England where they could be found in their wild state. It is many years since I saw a field of them but I believe they have by no means disappeared.

Most people in Oxford, in one way or another, worked for the University, for there was no Pressed Steel Works or Morris Motors then. If you worked in a shop or laundry, a bank or an accountant's office, or bookshop, those businesses would rely to no small extent on the University. So, in a way, almost everybody's livelihood rested on the money brought into Oxford by the University. Other than that, we were in our early years not conscious that it influenced our lives.

There were of course, benefits which were not apparent. For instance, education was of a higher standard in Oxford than in many Midland towns and as so many people catered in some way for 'The Gentlemen' food and cooking were of a high standard. Superb trifles with real cream, charlotte russe, castles of jelly made in moulds with fruit arranged decoratively were common at parties, for the parents of my school friends had either learned about these things from college kitchens where many of the men earned their livings or had been taught by those who worked in a college. This was not everyday food, but at christenings, weddings and parties, people showed off their skill and prosperity, and knew and appreciated good food and wine, for the odd bottle of vintage port or claret was often bestowed by someone 'up at the University' for one service or another.

When I was eight years old my mother—who had much more enterprise than my father and who was ever looking out for opportunities for her children—answered an advertisement in the *Oxford Times* for choristers at St Michael's at the North Gate. I was not aware I had a 'voice' although we had family sing-songs round the piano, but I suppose my mother realised I had and as the choristers at St Michael's had free education at what was regarded as one of the best schools in Oxford, a private school called Bedford House, and as Mother wanted me to have the best possible education, here was a chance of getting something better than my parents could readily afford.

I was given voice trials at home by Mr Drayton, the choir-master, and was accepted as a chorister, younger than any before, as nine was the usual commencing age. So for almost a year, although in the choir as a probationer, I went to the Central School at sixpence per week, to improve my education and acquire sufficient knowledge to enter Bedford House. It was at the Central School that I won my first prize 'for reading'. I sang my first song in public at a Band of Hope meeting. I was about seven years old. It went as follows:

> I'll be a soldier Daddy,
> Off to war I'll go
> Marching along with the boys so gay
> To fight old England's foe.

> Always I'll do my duty,
> Always be brave and true,
> I'll fight for King and Country
> And the Red, White and Blue.

The love of God, King and Country was our traditional upbringing. We were, I suppose, indoctrinated but it served us well and brought this country through two world wars.

We attended Sunday School and at the Band of Hope meetings plays were performed showing the evils of strong drink. Drunkenness was a common sight as pubs were open all day and men and women would be drunk by lunch-time. Through the efforts of the Band of Hope, people were induced to 'sign the pledge', by which they pledged themselves never to drink intoxicating beverages. People who signed the pledge were presented with little badges. They sang a hymn which went something like this:

> Many strands together make a strong rope,
> Many hearts united make a Band of Hope.
> We are out to slay the dragon who is helping Eng-
> land's foe,
> By the Grace of God we'll do it—and the drink
> shall go.

The Salvation Army did much good work, too, in this direction. Its bands played in the streets and the crowds were invited to 'throw a penny on the drum'. There were German bands too, which also played in the streets; they disappeared with the outbreak of war in 1914 and never returned. There was a song about these bands:

> Has anyone seen a German Band,
> German Band, oh! how grand,
> I've been looking around all upon my own.
> I've searched every street both near and far
> Near and far, Yah! Yah! Yah!

23

I want my Fritz what plays twiddly bits
On the big trombone.

Then there were the barrel-organs, some with monkeys on top. My old grandmother (Mother's mother) who had a general store and a very large yard, which in her prosperous days had housed carriages and stabled horses, now housed dozens of barrel-organs and the organ-grinders hired them out by the day and also hired barrows to take round various things like fruit and vegetables.

In her shop she sold cold bread-pudding and thick twists of black tobacco which people chewed. She sold snuff and pickled onions and small pokes of tea and sugar mixed, for a penny; for the people of St Thomas's were poor and the neighbourhood, which at one time had been prosperous, had become something of an over-crowded slum. These mean streets occupied a site which had in past centuries been one of the finest architecturally in the kingdom. For around here was Oseney Abbey, with its beautiful outbuildings along the waterside—one of the grandest monastic piles of England and the first cathedral in Oxford.

Housing in Henry Road, Alexandra Road, Helen Road— all named after members of Queen Victoria's family—and in the new streets adjacent was very superior to that in older parts of Oxford like St Thomas's, St Ebbes and, the strangely named 'Jericho' area, but we were not very conscious of it as we kept more or less to our attractive near-country locality.

II

We moved to North Street in Oxford when I was eight years old. The move to this larger house was necessary as the family had grown. The house was modern, with a bathroom—which, in those days, was the height of luxury. Very many houses in Oxford had no running water or inside lavatory.

My father was a very house-proud man, insisting on furniture and fittings of quality and taste. The house itself was one of only four in a nice position in North Street, facing the 'river' which branches off from the Thames to rejoin it after Osney Lock. I would spend whole days, wearing old shoes to avoid cutting my feet, paddling, fishing with a net and making traps for minnows and bullheads by building ponds on the side of the stream with mud and stones into which the fish—tempted with a piece of bread—would swim. The art was to block up the entrances quickly once there was a fish in the 'trap'. I fished too, with rod and line for gudgeon, dace, roach, perch and pike. Occasionally I would fry gudgeon for one of my friends. Many people considered them to be good eating.

I became particularly skilled at catching gudgeon with a ball of paste about the size of a small pea. The gudgeon's mouth is underneath its head, so one watched the bait and as soon as it disappeared one snagged the line as the fish covered the bait. Older folk fishing with a float were nowhere near as successful, and with a bit of luck one could, very occasionally, sell a few gudgeon for a halfpenny or even a penny or two as they are excellent bait used by pike fishermen.

My father was a keen fisherman and had plenty of rods and tackle, so I could usually find what I wanted among his things. He was keen on country life generally and would walk all day in the country, covering fifteen or twenty miles.

It was on one of these walks that he bought a raffle ticket in a country pub. There was great excitement at home some weeks later when he received a postcard stating that he had won a prize—a store pig. He described how he would deal with it. 'A store pig is a big one,' he declared, 'so we will salt some of it and have lovely ham to last us all the winter.'

Father together with my uncle set out to walk some ten miles to collect the pig, stopping for refreshment at almost every pub on the way. Arriving at the farm they were shown a sow with a litter of pigs and the farmer said they could choose any one—visions of ham for the winter faded out, but a tasty young pig was still a prize worth having. My father instructed my uncle to go into the pen, which was a sea of mud and muck, to get the pig, while he himself leaned over the fence, making encouraging and derisory remarks as my uncle floundered in the muck, chasing one piglet after another with little success. Father was something of a dandy and sported a straw boater with a gay ribbon. Leaning over the fence, full of beer and excitement and waving his arms he knocked off his boater, which the old sow immediately began to eat. The last he saw of his hat was a piece of the ribbon hanging out of the sow's mouth.

Ultimately the largest of the litter was secured and put into a sack, which got heavier and heavier as they trudged the long miles home. It was late at night when they got back to Oxford and they decided the best thing to do with the pig was to put it into my uncle's garden for the night. By the next morning it had eaten all his young cabbages. They took it to a local butcher for slaughter and we had half, my uncle the other half. It was, in size, little more than the joint we would normally buy for our household of nine. It was delicious, but my father declared that the pig he had taken alive to the butcher had been much larger than the one he got back.

For years Father would tell the story of the pig eating his hat and roar with laughter at his own idiosyncrasies. His high spirits and sense of fun made him a great companion, although they must often have maddened my Mother. 'I could build a house if I had the tools,' he would say; but in fact he was helpless as a practical man about the house and could not put a washer on a tap. He was entirely without ambition. Such people are blessedly happy.

I walked every weekday (Monday to Friday) from North Street, which is in West Oxford (just past the station), to choir practice in a room in New Inn Hall Street near the centre of the town. Oxford still had horse-drawn trams, but all children walked to school, some having to walk miles, and men walked to work.

A familiar sight was to see the whole street thickly covered with straw outside a house in which someone was seriously ill, and one saw it also outside the Court House at the time of the Oxford Assizes. This deadened the noise of the horse-drawn traffic and ensured a measure of quiet within the house, but it filled me with awe. Such measures would be quite useless today with aircraft crashing through the sound-barrier and so on.

We had to be at choir practice punctually by eight a.m. which continued until nine a.m. when we walked to Bedford House School in Walton Street in all weathers. We also had choir practice at eight p.m. each Friday evening with the full choir, as the men did not attend the morning practices.

Each Sunday there were morning and evening services and once a month a service for children on Sunday afternoon conducted by the Vicar, the Rev. Mansell Merry. The children's services on Sunday afternoons were extremely popular. The Vicar was a splendid preacher with a love of children. Such a fine man; I will never forget him!

Once he told us a story of God walking in the Garden of Eden stopping at each flower and asking its name. He went to

27

one flower and said, 'What is your name?' 'Rose' was the reply. Another answered, 'Lily', and so on. Then he stopped to look at a very small beautiful blue flower. 'And what is your name?' God asked. Sadly the flower whispered in a shy little voice, 'I forget.' 'Never mind,' said God. 'But forget me not!' So the flower was known ever afterwards as 'Forget-me-not'.

St Michael's choir was considered one of the best in Oxford and this, together with the outstanding ability and personality of the Vicar, attracted large congregations.

Bedford House School—regarded in its day as equal in everything but size to the Oxford High School—is now closed but the premises are still in Walton Street, much as they were in my schooldays. We had 'overspilled' into the 'shop' next door, the ceiling of which was covered with balls of blotting paper, for we had a disgusting sport of chewing blotting paper and placing it on the end of a ruler, in order to flick it on to the ceiling where it stuck. For variety we sometimes flicked it on to the back of someone's head.

Altogether there were four classes and a total of under one hundred pupils. 'Guts' was the headmaster, a character revered by many old boys. He was so-called by everyone on account of his large stomach; but on looking back I do not think it was particularly large. His name was Robinson and to me he was rather bullying and frightening, with a special torture of his own: he would clench his fist and with his knuckles beat a rapid tattoo on one's shoulder. But he was a great teacher as well as a disciplinarian and, as the reputation of his school depended on the success in examinations of his pupils, he saw to it that we worked. Many leading Oxford citizens agree he was a remarkable man and we 'old boys' of Bedford House owe much to him. In particular he instilled in us a strong sense of duty, for if any of us did not measure up to the high standard expected of us he would make that boy feel like a worm. He would lecture and shame him in front of the whole class. It was not kind but it worked.

A choir summer outing in those days was a special treat,

as few families went away for an annual holiday. A day's outing was a thrill; it took place on one of the beautiful decorative house-boats very similar to the few remaining college barges still moored on the banks of the Isis near Folly Bridge.

I believe the house-boats were hired from Salter Bros., who today run the steamers from Oxford. The house-boat was towed by horses as far as Nuneham Courtney. We had a piano on board and feasted and sang until we arrived at Nuneham and there sports were arranged. Of course, someone fell into the river regularly on each outing and this added to the fun of the day. Somehow it seemed the sun always shone, but in fact I imagine the weather then was much the same as now, although the winters were colder; I put this down to the fact that before the locks and weirs were enlarged and improved, the fields for miles around were flooded in winter and then froze, so that there were lakes of ice to make the whole atmosphere cold. Twice I saw the Thames frozen hard and photographs exist in some Oxford pubs of the roasting of an ox on the frozen river.

As choristers, each Ascension Day we went 'Beating the Bounds'. Each chorister, armed with a peeled willow wand, walked to the boundaries of the parish and beat with the sticks upon the spot indicated by the Vicar. As we beat, together with the party accompanying us, we yelled at the tops of our voices.

To make this old custom more interesting we were given all sorts of hazards, such as crawling through holes in walls and dropping down from the high wall of the Oxford High School. The ceremony terminated with a scramble for pennies—some hot—thrown to us by the Vicar and Wardens and the spectators. I never got much as I was small and not very good in a rough-and-tumble. Still in some parishes the custom has been to beat the boys themselves! The custom of beating the bounds is common to several European countries, but as far as I know, we at St Michael's at the North Gate were the only church carrying out the custom, although I know of several parishes in London and many in Scotland which still do so.

I suppose I must have been an attentive pupil at school—though I cannot remember working particularly hard—for somehow, over several years, I was top of the class. It follows that I was awarded a prize each year and I still have the books presented to me with their prize bookplates inscribed by the headmaster. Each month we had to take home a form for our parents to sign showing our progress; for many years my mother treasured the school cards of my progress but they are now lost.

It was fun to be one of a large family, but how Mother could keep the house clean, do all the washing and cook for nine people passes belief. At times we had a maid or other help but for long periods Mother did it all. I can still see the copper in which all our clothes were boiled, heated by a small coal or coke fire and the huge mangle, the handle of which I could hardly turn, with its large wooden rollers. The ironing was done with a series of flat irons heated on top of the kitchen range. The lines of washing reached right to the bottom of the garden, some eighty feet, with sheets and blankets as well as all our underclothes on them.

Every Sunday there was an enormous joint of beef or occasionally pork. These days one never sees such joints as a baron of beef or a roundbone of pork. Many butchers today would not know what a roundbone of pork is, but it was a well-known joint in Oxford.

> It's the roast beef of Old England
> That makes us what we are today.
> Hot on Sunday, cold on Monday,
> Tuesday and Wednesday too
> We turn it into Irish stew—

That was exactly the pattern. 'Hot on Sunday,' I never enjoyed it 'Cold on Monday' with pickles and mashed potatoes, but the 'Irish stew' was gorgeous and if there was a little left over we had it heated up for supper. The extra cooking did something to the meat and never have stews tasted better.

Yorkshire pudding, cooked under the joint to absorb the fat and rich juice from the meat, is something one never has now with the silly little joints of today, trimmed of fat and practically bloodless. Foreigners must often wonder why English people talk nostalgically of Yorkshire pudding when they are served such travesties of the real thing in our restaurants today. I refer to those horrid little individual puddings, tasting of nothing and feeling like cotton wool on the tongue.

A beef steak and kidney pudding made with real suet, a blackcurrant pudding boiled to perfection in such a way that the pudding was never soggy—the top was cooked by steam— were a gourmet's delight. The latter was so good that my father would have his served first, when his appetite was keenest: not for economy—like some families who would fill up with a pudding before the meat course, (because meat has always been expensive for working-class incomes)—but because he enjoyed it the more.

Vegetables fresh from our allotment, especially the peas and broad beans, were of a flavour now generally lost as a result of the use of artificial fertilisers. 'What lovely vegetables we do grow,' my father would proudly exclaim as he served us with our helpings. Food was good! Life was good! And we never wondered how much it cost or whether there was any sacrifice on our parents' part, as of course there was, to supply it.

Some weeks before Christmas we sat round the fire in the evenings preparing the fruit for the Christmas puddings. My mother made thirteen each year. I suppose the mixture worked out to this number. My father insisted that only the best real suet must be used and the raisins must be the real ones which had to be opened up one by one to remove the pips. 'No puddings are worth eating,' he declared, 'if not made with such raisins.' Seedless raisins were to him, new-fangled things of no merit.

Then we made the bread-crumbs, rubbing whole loaves through a grater. This was hard work and could be cruel on the fingers if one was careless, but it was all exciting and a foretaste of the pleasures of Christmas to come.

Christmas at home was an event, but its success depended in no small measure on the perfection of the puddings, for my father had a temper and was a perfectionist of the old Victorian school. A Christmas pudding must have just enough flour to hold it together—no more. It must turn out of the basin in perfect shape and gently crumble as the spoon entered it. If it had too much flour, his Christmas was ruined and so might ours be, because his temper, usually well under control, could be quite the reverse when he had had a few drinks, doubtless due to the fact that he was by no means a heavy drinker. If he had more than a few with his pals on Christmas Eve and a few more on Christmas morning, he might fly off the handle!

However, as a rule all was wonderful, if Mother had succeeded in keeping him at home on Christmas Eve; but of course, it was natural for him to want some fun. What peace was there for him at home with seven noisy children clambering all over him? All the same he loved children and had wanted a family of eight; but Mother decided that seven was enough and, like all women, she usually got her way in matters of importance.

Christmas Day arrived at last, with so much excitement that we could not sleep. I, at least, half-believed in Santa Claus and so, I think, did my sisters. We hung up our stockings the night before and in some miraculous way they were filled by the morning when we awoke in the dark, early hours and excitedly looked to see what we had 'been brought'. The stockings usually contained a few new pennies, an orange, and a large surprise packet or two wrapped in masses of paper which, when ultimately unwound, disclosed either nothing or some small top or novelty. We also had a main

Mother, aged nineteen—
'just an angel'

Father volunteered
under the Derby Scheme
(1914-1918 War)

(*Top*) Father (centre) punting on the Upper Thames

(*Middle*) This is the life! Father and Uncle Tom (centre) camping at Lechlade

(*Below*) Father's holiday balancing act—'his high spirits and sense of fun made him a great companion'

gift, too large for the stocking. I was keen on magic lanterns and shadowgraphs or toy theatres. We had little breakfast on Christmas morning, in order that we could the better enjoy Christmas dinner which we had at lunchtime.

Father would bring out all the decanters and fill them with wine which he had put aside over the year for this occasion. We were allowed a glass of port and perhaps a very small liqueur tasting of Parma violets or aniseed. He took pride in his array of decanters and glasses and he also arranged fruit and nuts, each variety in a separate bowl. I suppose this was necessary with seven hungry youngsters. At the great moment of the meal—his carving of the turkey—I prayed for a drumstick because if I got one I could only just manage to eat it and would feel wonderfully full all day. The Christmas pudding was covered with brandy and then there was the ceremony of warming a tablespoon with a taper and filling it with brandy until it caught alight. The tablespoonful was then poured over the pudding to ignite the brandy already over it. The curtains were drawn to give full effect to the magic of those blue flames.

We played with our new toys after dinner and, after a very small tea, for we were still full up, we had some songs at the piano. Father insisted that we all learned to play the piano and my sisters, particularly the two elder ones, were accomplished pianists. I was never any good but wanted to learn to play the banjo. Uncle Tom, my father's eldest brother—the great tycoon of the family, having become the managing director of an important clothing manufacturer—had in his youth played the banjo; he gave me his, a beautiful instrument, but I could never find anyone to tutor me.

Uncle Tom was our particular favourite. He loved Oxford and came to stay with us each year to attend the St Giles's Fair. He was generous with his half-crowns—a lot of money at that time, sufficient to see a boy through the two days of the Fair. My cousin Leonard and I were good pals, and my aunt came with my uncle. At one time Leonard had set his heart on possessing an airgun and had spoken of it to his father. One day he saw a gun in a brougham at my uncle's stable. It had evidently been left there by a factory hand, as the stable was near the entrance to the factory that my uncle managed at Crewe. I imagine the owner had been taking pot shots at the sparrows which abounded in the ivy and had left it on his return to work. Leonard ran into the house with it and said, 'Look Dad, this is the kind of gun I want.' He pulled the trigger, my uncle cried out and a feathered dart was sticking out of his left nostril. The gun had been left loaded. Uncle carried a tiny scar for the rest of his life, and Leonard never got his airgun.

More serious was the occasion when another uncle was showing a new shotgun to my Aunt Lizzie. 'My God!' she exclaimed, 'don't point it at me.' He pointed it at the wall, pulled the trigger and to their horror blew the wall surface to pieces!

Father had a good voice, and sang comic songs and the 'pop' music of the day such as 'Alexander's Ragtime Band', 'Baby Doll' and 'Following in Father's Footsteps'. Of the last:

> He's gone upstairs with a big fat gal
> I wish that I had one as well.

would sing Father, and 'Oh Alf!' exclaimed Mother, little realising that we did not understand the innuendo. But we shrieked with laughter, as we knew it was funny.

With a baby on his knee he would jog it up and down singing:

> Bumpety, bumpety, bumpety, bump,
> As if I was riding my charger,
> Bumpety, bumpety, bumpety, bump,
> Just like an Indian Rajah.
> And all the girls declare
> That I'm a gay old stager,
> Hi! Hi! clear the way

34

Here comes the galloping Major.

or:

My word if you're not off
I'll saw your leg off
And stick it on with beer
'Cos jam's too dear.

with variations:

And stick it on with glue
'Cos jam won't do.

or a lively song which went:

Yesterday what do you think I did
I insured the missus for fifty quid.
When I look at the policy, I think
Here's a terrible case,
Stony broke—fifty quid
Staring me in the face.

I can always memorise both the words and the tune of a song when I have heard it once or twice and friends laugh at the 'rubbish' I can remember. If only I found quotations from the classics of literature as easy! But it was years before the classics meant much to me, and so my mind is full of these extraordinary jingles.

Once my interest was aroused I could memorise anything, so that certain chapters, read from the Bible at the time I was a chorister have remained for ever in my mind. I can even quote long passages, but why these particular ones, I do not know.

Such trifles as the following from the reverse side of a box of England's Glory matches remain in my mind from

I suppose around 1915; it said 'To be sung to the tune of 'Sister Susie's sewing shirts for soldiers':

> Morland's make their matches "England's
>   Glory"
> Their marvellous manufactury is making
>   millions more
> Most matches make men mutter
> As they fizzle and they splutter
> Morland's matches match in brilliancy
> A monstrous meteor.

Both Father and Mother were circumspect and never allowed a word out of place in front of the children. Even when really angry, Father would very rarely swear. His oath vocabulary, voiced only after I grew up, was limited to 'damn and blast', never anything else. His mother, my grandmother, was a very regal figure and it was said that she was never heard to swear until she hit her thumb with a hammer and 'Oh! bugger!' she exclaimed to everyone's amazement. I cannot ever remember hearing my mother swear, and sex simply did not exist in our home. I would watch two or three babies being bathed and from time to time I was sent away because another was to be born, but I never connected the events. Even when my eldest sister and I were sent to fetch Nurse Watts because a baby was arriving, we only knew Mother was ill. We went with a note from North Street to Marlborough Road—a distance of about a mile and a half each way—for this emergency. No telephones were available for most people then.

When the Great War started in 1914 not one of the children in our family was fourteen years of age and as Father volunteered under the Derby scheme when he was called up it left us without any income other than the miserable and disgraceful family allowances of that war.

So we almost starved, not so much because of the shortage of money but because food became scarce as the submarines sank the shipping, and in the first years there was no such thing as rationing. It was obviously impossible for Mother to leave us all to join the long queues for food. I would wait for hours to get one ounce of butter or margarine for her and would go to the skin-yard where, if I was lucky, I would sometimes get a few sheep's trotters to make a stew. We ate rice when we could get it, instead of potatoes which were extremely scarce, and we bought soup squares. These last were compressed cubes of brown powder which were crumbled into hot water. Once rationing started we had the advantage, as the rations for a large family were sufficient in bulk, although possibly insufficient as regards vitamins and true nourishment over a long period.

Times were hard and the Oxford & Bucks Light Infantry was practically wiped out. About six thousand Oxford boys were killed, so that almost every family was bereaved. To these must be added the young undergraduates, about three thousand of whom were also killed. The total population of Oxford was only around 50,000 so that, assuming half were women, the total number of men of military age could not have been much greater than the number killed.

Oxford was an interesting and safe place to be during the war; only once do I remember taking shelter under the table when there was a Zeppelin raid in the Loughborough area many miles away. We would go to the station and watch the train loads of troops depart; later the Belgian refugees arrived and train loads of wounded men who were carried off to the Base hospital. Boys pestered the soldiers for badges and buttons, which they collected, and the wounded, suffering as they were, were extremely good-humoured and kind about it. There was a prisoner of war camp on Hinksey Hill and trenches and ranges upon which soldiers trained. I found a grenade and took it to pieces entirely failing to realise that it could go off. It's a wonder I am alive.

Even at that age the tragedy and pathos were not lost on me and we had fears about Father who, we all knew, would be a pretty useless soldier. We may have underestimated him

37

in this but none of us was ever really to know, as he never spoke of his few war experiences in the Balloon Section of the Army. I remember Mother's tears as his pathetic letters arrived home and I know he was something to do with Kite balloons. He said he once went up in one. Of one thing only am I certain—he did not like it! So we were all glad and relieved when the war was over and we could return to normal.

The war was followed by a terrible flu epidemic in 1918. Most of us caught it and many of our friends died. There seemed to be funerals every day.

The landlord had put up our house for sale and Father, being away, could not bid for it, so after a time we had notice to quit. It was all very upsetting but worked out for the best as we moved to a larger house in Walton Street, much nearer the centre of Oxford. A bathroom and two water closets now —we were moving up!

My eldest sister started work as a junior clerk trainee at the high-class grocers and wine merchants, Grimbley Hughes, in Cornmarket Street (alas! another Oxford landmark no longer in existence) at a starting wage of two-and-six per week.

I was anxious to begin working for a living and a seed had been sown when the Rev. C. A. Smith, who succeeded the Rev. Mansell Merry as Vicar of St Michael's at the North Gate, said that, if any of us wanted to go into a library, his friend was the head librarian of the Bodleian and would give special consideration to anyone he recommended. I knew I was something of a favourite of his and that he would speak for me, so I asked him to do so and was duly appointed a junior assistant at eleven-and-six per week. I took ten shillings home for Mother each week and felt truly rich with one-and-six to spend.

I soon got into trouble at Bodley for the extraordinary offence of carrying a battery torch in my pocket, which was against the rules of the library. Unfortunately it was accidentally switched on in my pocket and the light was seen through the cloth by a senior woman assistant. Women were introduced into Bodley as a wartime measure. I lost a half-day's holiday. Of course we were not allowed to carry matches and this made sense, but what harm could a battery torch do? I think they still regarded them as infernal machines which could set fire to the library—surprising in a seat of learning! One thing it taught me early on, was never to work under a woman, and although I consider myself very much a feminist, in my experience women are not good at the top and the fact that most women prefer working under a man confirms this. Yet one's success is often due to the loyalty and industry of women; I know mine is for I have been particularly fortunate in this respect. Women I conclude make good 'seconds' but rarely the best 'firsts'.

We worked from nine a.m. until twelve noon and on 'night duty' again from six p.m. until eight p.m. As the streets were still blacked out we carried torches or wore luminous buttons when darkness had fallen. I did not see luminous buttons in the last war. They were about the size of a florin and if put into the sunlight during the day, shone with a light-blue glow in the dark, so that by wearing them people did not bump into one another. I suppose they were radioactive and possibly quite dangerous, but no one thought about that or knew anything of radioactivity then.

A copy of every book published under the Copyright Act is supplied to the Bodleian Library and they all have to be catalogued and placed in their correct positions on the shelves. The latter was the particular duty of the junior assistants, coupled with the fetching of books for the readers. No book could be taken out of the library but had to be read and studied on the premises.

The Radcliffe Camera then housed the more recent publications and when I was on 'night duty' at the Radcliffe Camera, I lived in fear that I would have to fetch books from the basement. There are two floors of books below the surrounding lawn. This is a creepy, eerie place of what seemed to me, at that time, to be of vast dimensions, with a metal floor like a grating on which were avenues of bookcases which ran on wheels. As one went down these dark avenues the cases tended to 'creep out' on one and cut off one's retreat from 'anything' or anyone which one imagined was there. If the bogeys were imaginary, there was always the likelihood of some practical joker pushing a case and howling like a banshee. The junior assistants were a pretty lively bunch and up to every kind of mischief; more than one senior assistant had a heavy book fall on his head as he pushed open a door. The 'trap' had been set off by a junior for another junior but occasionally the joke misfired. The punishment depended on the sense of humour of the injured party.

One thing has since struck me as being very curious. Amongst literally millions of books, the older boys always knew the more pornographic ones and the pages which were 'blue'. Some old, very old publications are, to put it mildly, 'curious' and if books can corrupt, then librarians and book-sellers should be moral perverts, but the reverse seems to be the case. Here is food for thought...

When I was serving as a committee member of a Special Committee (1968-1969) of the Arts Council* to examine the laws relating to pornography no evidence emerged that books had any corrupting influence—rather the reverse. Books may disgust but seem to have no adverse effect on normal people. I pointed out that to condemn a bookseller, or to seize his stock because some individual or group considered certain books harmful, was as stupid and unfair as condemning a chemist for selling aspirin which, taken in sufficient quantity, is poison.

I recently read that one librarian has taken the 'Billy Bunter' books off the shelves as they ridicule fat boys and encourage the slim to deride or bully fat people. So it has ever been. Some well-meaning 'do-gooder' can find a reason to ban almost everything published. Such people mean well, but get the whole thing out of perspective.

When I was reading Mardrus's translation of the *Arabian*

* Fully recorded in '*The Obscenity Laws*' published by André Deutsch.

Nights, a reverend professor of Arabic caught me in the act. 'Are you reading that?' he asked. Rather fearfully I said, 'Yes.' 'That's all right,' he replied, 'it's good schoolboy dirt, I let my son read it. It will do you no harm.' I am convinced he was right, and a good open approach is better than the reverse, which leads to dirty minds.

One of my early sweethearts had two elder sisters and they had boy friends much older than myself. They would strum on the piano and shock everyone as they parodied well-known classics. 'I dreamt that I dwelt in marble halls' became:

> I dreamt that I tickled my grandfather's balls
> With a little sweet oil and a feather ... etc.

Years afterwards a sophisticated young woman of my acquaintance who had overheard the words sung by these fellows was staying with an elderly friend and her husband. The husband described with great gravity his ministrations to a cherished old grandfather clock. It was not working well, so he had applied 'a little sweet oil with a feather'. My friend went into hysterics and to this day has never been able to explain her uncontrollable mirth.

One man's classics of literature are another man's pornography, so no one man or group can competently act as censors. Censorship of books is a big problem and a book that disgusts or annoys some people can, at the same time, be a valuable piece of literature. People have been persecuted more for publishing books on religion than for pornography. The question remains, should we have a 'free-for-all' or is some form of control workable?

Bodley was indeed an education—fascinating, bewildering—and an experience never to be forgotten. The seniors were cultured, tolerant and most kind to all the juniors and we respected them, in spite of our pranks. The head librarian reprimanded a junior assistant one day for dropping a book. 'You must,' he said, 'exercise due care and not be careless in handling books.' A few days later the librarian himself dropped a book in front of this same junior assistant. Unabashed he said, 'My boy, I would like you to learn from this practical example the working of the force of gravity.' I learned a useful lesson: the 'boss' is never wrong.

I was studying at night school, having private tuition and generally continuing my education, but I could not see myself as a librarian for life, so I asked my parents to apprentice me to a local bookseller. This they did. It meant our signing an indenture to bind me for five years during which time I would earn ten shillings a week for the first year with a two shillings a week annual increase. A twenty pound deposit was needed so, in effect, it took almost the whole of the first year to get back the amount of the deposit.

Just before I left the Bodleian Library I was awarded the First Curator's Prize, the highest merit award open to a junior assistant. When I was summoned to go to the head librarian, I thought I was in trouble, but I could not think which 'crime' had been discovered. My friend Lionel Harrison—later Sheriff of Oxford—was summoned with me. I remember clearly our washing and tidying ourselves up for whatever ordeal lay before us. We both thought we would get the sack, since otherwise we should not have been sent for.

I was staggered when I was awarded the First Curator's Prize and Harrison received the Second, because such a recognition was usually given to the most senior boy and I received it with less than a full year's service. It was indeed a great honour to have my name painted on a board listing all prize winners.

The booksellers' apprenticeship system which I was now to experience had much merit, as we were really taught the trade by conscientious booksellers of high ethical standard and with sound business methods. In these days such low wages would, I suppose, be regarded as exploitation. Knowing the benefits, however, I have over the years tried—so far without success—to institute something on rather similar lines: a more modern student scheme to take the place of the old apprenticeships to bookselling. I envisage three years training with qualified booksellers, linked with tuition and examinations. A scale of wages during the period should be agreed and, finally, courses in management should be available. The trade and public would, I am sure, benefit by such courses, which after all are common practice in several European countries.

The scheme will eventually come, but precious years are being wasted. A sound initial training in any trade or profession is an obvious advantage and I, for one, am grateful to the apprenticeship system and truly feel I had an advantage over those who started in bookselling as junior assistants. They did not usually have as much tuition and were not moved around, as were we apprentices, to gain experience in all departments.

III

I had an Uncle Baker who was chief clerk at Blackwell's in Oxford, so by arrangement I went to see him to discuss the prospects for myself in bookselling. He gave me good advice and suggested J. Thornton & Son, a University bookseller, one of Blackwell's 'rivals' in The Broad, because it was smaller and would give me an opportunity of experience in all departments. I took his advice, little realising this was the beginning of a long and exciting career in bookselling.

My first 'desk' at Thornton's was simply a piece of thin wood which was supported at either end on a bookcase. It was covered by a sheet of cardboard and there I started to learn the 'mysteries' of bookselling, having promised in writing to 'keep my master's secrets'.

Boyhood days were over and fifty years would pass before I again had three weeks holiday at one stretch. Until then I had been quite a Huckleberry Finn, living and playing, with the river as my special domain. I would make rafts and occasionally find an old boat. Of course I should have drowned, as did quite a number annually. It was then, as now, vital to be able to swim to survive in Oxford, a city of rivers and canals. I could not swim correctly until my father made me have lessons when I was eight years old; but I had been jumping into water, twenty feet deep or more, long before and was quite at home with my dog-paddling. I could also surface dive, though I could not dive off the bank. So I learned to be almost as much at home under water as on the surface and this is most valuable in an emergency, for some quite good swimmers drown when capsized, as they lose their heads when under the surface.

I fell out of trees, and once had concussion. I was roasting (burning to be more accurate) a potato and, while waiting for it to cook in the bonfire, I climbed a tree, slipped and was carried home concussed. A curious thing is that I could not afterwards eat a potato cooked in its jacket without feeling sick! Accidents of this kind were everyday occurrences. My sister Ethel was nearly drowned, as I describe later, and we all had various narrow escapes.

Although Father was such a keen river man, I cannot remember him going swimming, unless one recalls the summer day in Jersey when, fully clothed with trouser-bottoms turned up, he went off with a shrimping net. Always impatient, he went out among the rocks further and further. The tide goes out a long way there and in parts you can be cut off as the tide swirls around various rocks. Father was up to his neck before he could retrace his steps, but fully clothed and wearing his straw boater he went on fishing.

Father never missed a Henley Regatta. He loved 'The River' and many times he, with my uncles, camped near the Round House at Lechlade on the Upper Thames in the summer vacations. Once we were off for a day on the river Cherwell and the weather was uncertain. My father wanted to wear his new straw boater but was anxious not to spoil it in the rain, so he took two. The new one he wore when the sun shone and the other each time the clouds appeared. This pantomime went on all day.

Towards evening we passed under a rather low branch of a tree which swept the boater—of course, he was wearing the new one at the time—off his head. We watched it float away. It was at such times that Father was most funny, laughing at himself, an amusing mixture of fury, anguish and fun.

Father would rather poach than fish according to regulations. He made himself a rod just three feet long in order that he could trawl and no one see what he was up to. We had boatloads of fish to give away and by trawling we caught the largest. He would set eel lines at dusk and tie them to the reeds at the side of the river. 'How will you know where to find them in the morning?' I asked. 'Oh! that's easy! They are just opposite that cow,' he replied.

When he came into a little money, after an insurance policy had become due, he bought a car from an undergraduate. It was a Singer with a curious box of 'dog wheels' not cog wheels over the back axle. This caused endless worry and expense. He had me taught to drive and he himself had lessons, but he was hopeless. The main trouble was that he could never stop. One day—and this is hardly credible— we were out nearing Woodstock with father at the wheel, when we saw about twenty mules and donkeys all over the road. I suppose they belonged to gipsies or a travelling circus. My father, at speed, dodged in and out and miraculously missed hitting any animal—more, I swear, because of their nimbleness than his skill. He was extremely proud of his prowess but it never occurred to him to brake. When trying to stop at the house he would usually manage it within five hundred yards more or less. When one was driving out of the garage, the entrance of which faced a brick wall, it was necessary to 'crawl' out in order to give the wheel maximum turn, but he went into the wall head on without even beginning to turn! He simply roared with laughter and would never admit that he was no driver. This was both a maddening and fascinating trait in his make-up.

Once he sent for a lawn-mower, mail order, and when it arrived it was necessary to fix on the handle. He wrestled with it for hours and at last got it to cut the grass if it was pulled but not pushed. He declared, of course, that 'the machine was wrongly constructed in the first place'.

He was rather fascinated by mail order, so that when he once saw an advertisement, 'How to cure a red nose 2/6', he sent for the remedy although he did not suffer from this handicap. He received back a card saying 'Keep on drinking until it turns blue!'

Another incredible fact about my father is that on more than one occasion he pulled out his own teeth with pliers from the tool chest. Mother would tell us the next morning about it and say he had had terrible tooth-ache and took a few brandies to give him Dutch courage to pull the tooth out. He could evidently face this ordeal better than a visit to the dentist. One day he pulled out one of his eye teeth but the gap it left did not appeal to him, so he pushed the tooth, which had a long root, back into the socket from which he had extracted it. He kept it that way for several years.

In due time he had to have dentures and the dentist said, 'Have you any dentures at present?' 'No,' he replied, 'unless you call this a denture,' and he took out the tooth. The dentist said in a lifetime's experience he had never seen anything similar.

As children, my mother would pull out our loose first teeth by tying a cotton thread round them. This was quite usual in most homes.

Father was a staunch Conservative and, as children, we wore brooches bearing the face of the Conservative candidate. He named one of my sisters Primrose, after Primrose Day, the day of the Conservative Party. When we moved to Walton Street we lived exactly opposite Ruskin College which my father regarded as some kind of revolutionary establishment with no right to be called an Oxford College. Most nights we heard the 'Red Flag' being sung as we lay in bed. My father was infuriated by this evidence of rebellion against an order which he cherished.

Occasionally I would go into Ruskin College for a party or dance, because they let the hall for such occasions. Once I lost a girlfriend because I sang the 'Red Flag' with the rest. I sang merely for the joy of singing, having no political feelings, but from that day the girl would have nothing to do with me. It was a pity, because she was a good dancing partner and at that time dancing meant more to me than female company. Father, of course, sent me to dancing classes to be taught properly but later complained, I thought unreasonably, that I was 'always out dancing'.

Saturday night dances, entrance sixpence, were held regularly in a hall in the Clarendon Press Institute. We were experts at Old Time as well as the waltz, foxtrot and onestep and no dances during my whole life have equalled them. The 'posh' dances were held at the Masonic Hall and the Oxford Gymnasium, before the building of the Carfax Assembly Rooms. Most of these were club dances organised for the funds of the local rowing or cricket clubs. Entrance was one-and-six and to very special evening dress affairs, two-and six, refreshments extra, comprising usually a glass of lemonade made with lemonade powder and a small iced cake.

Neither I nor my friends wanted or could afford intoxicating drinks but because of my high spirits more than one dancing partner thought I had had a few. The girls I met did not drink or go into pubs. Most were 'very respectable' and although we kissed and cuddled, few went much further; but we knew who the naughty ones were, as youth does not keep such things secret.

One is rather bored by the amount of sex in books nowadays so I will not enlarge on this topic. Suffice it to say that if we were 'good' it was because we had had instilled into us common decency, the danger of unwanted babies, disease and a fate much worse, DISGRACE. To bring trouble and disgrace on one's parents was the unpardonable crime. My sisters say Mother told them the only safe precaution was 'No', but I think they were married before she spoke of sex to them. I do not think any adult spoke of it to me. I cannot remember having any sex instruction until I read a book entitled *What a Young Man Ought to Know*, and that was after I had started work. It was enough to frighten anyone off—which was, I suppose, its aim.

The Rev. C. A. Smith, Vicar of St Michael's explained to us choristers the absurdity of swearing and the derivation of certain swear words. 'Bloody', he explained, was almost certainly taken from a sacred oath 'By Our Lady', which became slurred as time went by to 'bloody'. He never told us the meaning of the four letter words, although some of the boys asked him. He concluded that it was just as stupid to say 'Oh damn!' as it was to say, 'Oh potatoes!' My expletives then, as now, were 'Christchurch' and 'to hell with it'. I occasionally still come out with 'honour bright'—obviously I was influenced by the 'goody-goody' book of that title and it became part of my vocabulary.

On the outskirts of Oxford—for instance, in the village of Cumnor—'bugger' is almost a term of endearment. 'Come on, you old bugger' they call when it is your turn to throw a dart. One soon gets used to it but one must resist the picking up of a habit. Remember how shocked people were to see in print the four letter word in D. H. Lawrence's *Lady Chatterley's Lover*. But this is commonly used in the Berkshire villages and has been since Chaucer's time at least. 'Oh he's a proper c..t,' they say.

It reminds me of the story of the Berkshire farmer who managed to send his son to a public school. The boy writing home a year or so later wrote, 'I am sharing a room with a proper count.' 'There,' said the old farmer, 'a whole year at one of the best public schools and the boy still cannot spell properly!'

Freeborn was our local butcher and his shop, at the corner of Henry Road, had stables at the rear and huge tubs of meat in salt water. One of his men drove a small butcher's cart round the Oxford villages—or more accurately the Berkshire villages, because if one lives in West Oxford, the country over the river is Berkshire—and he would take me with him to look after the horse by holding the reins as he delivered the meat in the cottages. He sang all the way, reading the words from a 'Song Sheet'. He knew all the popular songs that had come from America at that time: 'Are you from Dixie?', 'Carolina Moon', 'On the Mississippi', 'Get out and get under'.

My reward for helping him was indeed a treat, a packet of biscuits and a bottle of stone ginger at The Vine or The Bear and Ragged Staff in Cumnor village. No ginger-beer has since been so sweet or had the flavour of that sold in the stone screw-top bottles. Even the bottles are now collectors' items and can be bought for around seven-and-six each in some Oxford antique shops. A bottle of stone ginger in those days cost a penny.

My father and many local people used the expression 'It's a stone ginger' for 'It's a certainty', referring especially to a horse which would certainly win. I have not heard the expression elsewhere and am not sure of its derivation, but I imagine that ginger-beer sold in stone bottles was more reliable than the variety drawn from the wood.

There are lots of local expressions which, from time to time, I still use. Every Oxford child and adult knew what a doctor meant when he said 'Now quilt' (to swallow as if you had something in your mouth), but few people have heard the expression outside Oxford and think it very odd.

Berries are 'gogs' in good old Oxford slang—rasgogs, strawgogs, goosgogs. 'I ain't got any bleeding clean socks,' complained a small boy. 'How many times have I told you not to say 'ain't?' replied his mother. A schoolmaster took up the same point by quoting, when a boy said 'I ain't got no pen':

> I have no pen
> Thou hast no pen
> He has no pen
> We have no pens
> You have no pen
> They have no pens ...

The grammatical point was entirely lost on the boy who replied, 'Then who's got all the bleeding pens?' This Oxford use of oaths and slang was common among the boys at St Frideswide's School in West Oxford, which I attended before I was eight years old, as it is on the boundary of Oxford and Berkshire and many pupils came there from the nearby villages and farms. Youth is influenced by environment, particularly regarding speech, and one quickly acquires what is known as an Oxford accent in a high school environment. But I have never entirely lost some of the Berkshire brogue, people ask me 'Do you come from Somerset?' or, 'Are you West Country?'. I suppose the words of the song:

> Oi be nigh on ninety-seven
> Born and bred in dear old Devon

would sound much the same to foreign ears if spoken by a Devonian or a Berkshire man. I find few people can identify the Berkshire brogue.

Wytham is a particularly picturesque village, where we often went in the butcher's cart along a lane, a distance of about one mile. Wytham 'Lane' was actually a main road to the village with gates across it at regular intervals, perhaps six in all, to prevent cattle wandering from field to field. It was a nuisance to have to dismount to unlatch each gate and hold it open until the horse and cart passed through. A few beggars and tramps would try to pick up an odd copper by waiting at the gates, especially the first and the last, and opening them for you. Here I came across a most extraordinary thing. One old man at the first gate—a gipsy I think—would ask if you would like him to whistle up the rats for a penny. If you paid him this amount, he made a curious whistling, almost a hissing screech, through his teeth and lips and sure enough the rats began to appear from holes on the edge of Wytham Wood, as many as twenty or even more at certain times of the year. I have since wondered if this was a handed-down trick, probably known to gipsies, and could this possibly account for the story of 'The Pied Piper of Hamelin', making it a story actually based on fact?

The Thames and its tributaries are full of pike, perch and roach and these are the favourite fish angled for. In those days people would eat their catch; but nowadays when one sees fishermen pegged out along the banks, fishing in competition, all the catch is ultimately returned to the water, many surely injured for life. I cannot get much thrill out of this kind of fishing but to fish for salmon or trout, both delicious to eat, ah, that is a different matter! But there are no salmon and trout streams in Oxford, so one must sympathise with the fishermen, who enjoy fishing for coarse fish. A day by the side of a river with rod and line has for them all the pleasure so lovingly described by Walton in his *Compleat Angler.*

I have often read in books of delicious pike dishes but whenever I have tasted pike it has had a terribly muddy flavour. Over the years I have mentioned this to various people and have received a variety of explanations, including the one that in olden days the fish were not served straight from the river but were placed in special ponds where they cleaned themselves over a period.

On one of our holidays, which we were spending in Austria, pike caught in the large lake, the Wörthersee, were a speciality and at last I looked forward to tasting pike properly prepared and marinaded. I saw the large fish being prepared and it was marinaded for two days and announced proudly on the menu as 'a speciality of the district'. What a let down!—to my palate it tasted exactly the same as a pike fresh from the Thames.

A small fresh perch, cleaned and skinned and left over-night in slightly salted water, is not unlike trout but with something of the texture of a Dover sole. Not bad! Trout are, of course, good eating. To some the best fish caught in British waters is what the Welsh people call a 'Sewen' (sea trout), delicious served hot or cold and preferred by many to salmon; but a freshly run Atlantic salmon is the King of Fishes, both as a sporting fish and as a food.

All my life, above all things, I wanted to fish for salmon, and through the kindness of my great friend Eric Bailey (President of the Booksellers' Association) my wish has been fulfilled and over several years I have enjoyed his hospitality and the joys and thrills of salmon fishing in the beautiful

Carmarthen waters. My great regret is that the Thames, which at one time was full of salmon, had none when I was a boy. The last salmon recorded killed in the Thames was on October 3rd, 1812.

IV

Every Oxford child of my generation remembers certain eccentrics, the most famous being 'Red-Headed Peter' and the 'British Workman'; the former regularly lectured in the street somewhere near the Martyrs' Memorial. The latter dressed for no known reason in old corduroy trousers fastened with a cord below each knee. He was, I understand, a member of the University, a clever man if I was correctly informed. Everyone remembers the one and only Jimmy Dingle who but recently died, aged eighty-four. Jimmy Dingle, 'The Reliable Top Hat man', appeared over very many years in the main thoroughfares of Oxford dressed in a tail-suit, white spats and gloves and a top hat. He paraded in this attire carrying sandwich-boards twenty by twenty-five inches.

It started I imagine, first as a good gimmick, which helped him to earn a living, but gradually his resplendent costume became notorious and Jimmy collected substantial amounts for many charities over many years, particularly for the Oxford Eye Hospital. If any man should have been honoured by the City or the University or even by the State, it was Jimmy Dingle. Jimmy was popular with everyone, so much so that his marriage attracted one of the largest crowds ever seen in Oxford. He and his bride received cheers equal to those received by Royalty. Jimmy was the last of the 'characters' I knew as a boy.

Children can be cruel and how it is that they can tease and call out at poor old beggars, tramps and mentally retarded people to a point where they lose control and feeling forced to retaliate, chase the miscreants instead of ignoring them, I never know. There were several quite extraordinary characters who were jeered at by the children, feared by them too, and teased, until they swore and perhaps gave chase, gesticulating wildly in their anger.

Two such were 'Rhubarb and Custard' who lived or camped out gipsy fashion in Ferry Hinksey Road. Who 'christened' them no one knows, but children would call out 'Rhubarb and Custard' and they would get madly angry and chase the children who, of course, found it fun in spite of their fear. Another was 'Cat's Milk' who came round bowed down by a yoke on which were suspended two large containers of milk. If the children jeered at him, crying out again and again 'Cat's Milk', he would drop his pails and chase them.

'Banana Kate' used to push a huge barrow—the sort barrow-boys use—of over-ripe bananas. She was a picture, as she wore long bloomers, plainly visible as she pushed the cart, which necessitated bending her body. In the St Giles's Fair she sold whelks, which reminds me of a character who similarly had two jobs. He sold the local newspaper, the *Oxford Times*, which came out once weekly, and during the week he sold winkles. He was usually drunk and would get confused crying out, '*Oxford Times*, penny half-a-pint, winkles penny each!'

'Old Dobbin', another well-known Oxford character, would sing 'The Farmer's Boy' year after year to the queue outside the theatre, but the most curiously named was 'Itchy Blowfly'. He too was a poor man, who lived in one of the huts in Ferry Hinksey Road. Not only were there such people to add zest to life but there were fascinating places too, such as Cooper's Marmalade Factory near the Station with its appetising smell of cooking marmalades and boxes of Seville oranges being unloaded. One day, when an orange fell out of a crate, the man said I could have it. What disappointment! Until then I had not realised that Seville oranges used in marmalade were practically inedible. The ice factory, too, was a fascinating place where huge blocks of ice were to be seen coming out straight from the freezing chambers.

Morrell's and Hall's breweries with their wonderful odour of hops and their beautiful dray horses, and the local blacksmiths shoeing horses were all sights and smells to enthral boys and girls. Near our home in North Street was Peasley's Yard, which was the large yard of the pub of the Osney Arms. It was here that at regular intervals they would slaughter and singe a pig and this had a macabre attraction, with the squealing of the pig, the smell of its burning hair and then the bestowing of its burnt toe nails. These last were regarded as delicacies by the boys and girls lucky enough to get them. They chewed them but I believe they were too tough to eat.

Then there was the Haunted Barn in Binsey Lane. Why it was haunted and by whom, I never learned, but we children hurried past it with furtive, backward glances. Similarly we feared the Wytham Bull. On any walk there was some excitement, some mischief to be up to, and always there were 'leaders' to encourage those of us who would have rather kept out of trouble. But it takes courage not to mind being thought a coward and all too often, lacking this courage, one was up to as much mischief as the rest! It was just such a circumstance which almost led to the death of my young sister.

Mother and Father had gone for a day's outing, or maybe just out for an hour or two, and cautioned my sisters not to go near the river. A regular caution this and as regularly ignored. Off my sisters went, but were obedient to the point that they did not paddle in the stream but took off their shoes and stockings and *pretended* to paddle in a large field. Two girl cousins of mine taunted them and said that 'they were going to paddle in the stream', and rather than be thought cowards my sisters paddled under the treacherous little bridge in Binsey Lane. On one side of the bridge the water is shallow and on the other quite deep, and the moss and weed make the floor of the bridge as slippery as ice. Seeing a little fish, my sister Ethel tried to catch it in her hand, slipped and was

56

quickly in deep water. Neither could swim and the last she remembered was seeing her elder sister, Doris, up to her neck trying to reach her. The cries of my cousins on the bank brought, I think, a postman and baker to the scene, one of whom rescued Ethel while the other successfully applied artificial respiration. My father rewarded the rescuer with a gold watch.

My eldest sister, Hilda, was dropped overboard from a punt by our young housemaid when less than two years old and I have lost count of the number of times I fell in and had narrow escapes.

The family survived such mishaps somehow; but our youngest sister, Olive Gertrude, died of a heart disease when she was only thirteen years old. Mother and Father grieved for her all the rest of their lives, and so, to this day, do my sisters and I. It is strange to think she would now be almost sixty years of age, had she lived, because we still see her as a child.

By an extraordinary coincidence while I was writing this chapter, my wife and I attended a theatre party followed by a dinner given in New Zealand House by the Martini people, where we sat at a table with Miss Jennie Lee, (then Minister of State, Department of Education and Science), and nine others. A hundred and fifty to two hundred people were present. In talking to a man who sat next to my wife, Oxford came into the discussion and suddenly he said, 'You're not Tommy Joy, are you?' On hearing that I was indeed, he continued: 'When I was a boy of fifteen I was very much in love with your little sister, Olive, who died.' I was very moved and vaguely remembered a young boy who used to bring her flowers when she was ill. It was he!

In that large, happy, excited assembly I was suddenly back with the poignant memory of my parents' suffering as they watched so prolonged an illness, seeing little Olive, a young bonny girl, slowly waste away over the years, knowing there was no hope of recovery. I saw again my little sister's gentle smile. She had a happy nature and to the last was confident of recovery. It suddenly seemed a sad, small world.

V

The great event of the year for Oxford children was, and still is, St Giles's Fair. It is the largest fair held in a street in this country. The whole of the wide thoroughfare of St Giles, in the centre of Oxford, is given up to it for two days each year and, although from time to time some of those well-intentioned busybodies who want to change everything have endeavoured to have the Fair moved to meadows outside the city, it continues to be held in the street.

As children we had two days extra school holiday specially for the Fair; adults and young alike so looked forward to it that we went on the Sunday preceding the opening to see the large, gay traction engines, caravans and trailers in the station yard or in the lanes around Oxford, where they waited ready to rush to St Giles at the permitted early hour on the Monday. The first roundabout to get going was first 'in business'.

I recall, as does everyone born in Oxford, these annual fairs, and people of my age remember nostalgically the magic of the great roundabouts with their wonderful ornamental organs with figures striking drums and cymbals, all worked by steam. Music and animation were controlled by a punched card system similar to a pianola roll.

There were great gondolas scorching round over the humps in the track, which made the girls cling to their boy friends, screaming; there was the cake-walk and giant 'steam' boats which spun round full circle, literally upside down as they turned around. There too, was 'the mat' (helter-skelter), on which you slid down having first climbed to the top inside the tower, still as popular today as then—as are the 'galloping horses'; and of course conspicuous at every fair was the 'big wheel'. But the 'bicycles' have gone. This was a kind of roundabout made up of many bicycles. The 'power' was the fast power of thirty to fifty cyclists all trying to go like mad. The combined efforts of all on the roundabout could make it a hair-raising ride! Cycling was a novelty then and few possessed bicycles of their own.

Today's canned music has not the allure of the old organs, and electric light has not the glamour or the fascination of the old naphtha flares which, in my boyhood, were used to illuminate the stalls. The hot paraffin smell and the lighting up of these flares at dusk held a special attraction for a boy.

Coconut shies, dart stalls, shooting ranges were then much the same as at fairs today but the side-shows were much more glamorous to a less sophisticated public. Here were the loveliest creatures I had ever seen: dancing girls on a stage, in front of a back-cloth, to attract you in, generally to see a new invention—moving pictures. The earliest films we saw were at the Fair in the side-shows and these were amongst the first ever made; cinemas were still unknown. These early short films were apparently shot in pouring rain, but in fact this rain effect was caused by poor equipment and doubtless the films were pretty worn. But those dancing girls! ... I suppose I was growing up.

As we reached our early teens the Fair had an even greater thrill for it was customary for us to go armed with powder-puffs and boxes of cheap, perfumed powder. Almost the whole population of Oxford paraded up and down the Fair the whole evening and the art was, having selected your 'victim', to powder her face. She would lean back to avoid the powder and then you embraced her. The kissing of all the girls you had always wished to kiss, some of whom you singled out for weeks ahead, ready for the great occasion, was indeed the high spot of the evening. Later, the Chief

Constable—I think it was—took action, because the Ambulance Service had to deal with several casualties when powder had got into people's eyes and some older women complained of being kissed by strange men.

So powder was stopped just when I had perfected the art, for having lost several powder puffs—the girls would grab them, given a chance—I had a nice puff tied to my wrist. Without the powdering, the kissing stopped and the 'improvement' was remarkable; from that day people of both sexes dealt one another stunning blows from the handles of 'ticklers', a brush fixed to the end of a 'stick' made of rolled-up wall-paper. This was a painful procedure and one wished the authorities had left things as they were. Once the kissing stopped the Fair was never the same, and today, with its gambling-machines, strip-tease and canned music, doubtless the authorities consider it 'an improvement' on the previous manifestations of our natural urges. Unnecessary restraint so often leads to worse alternatives but many in authority never learn this lesson.

Father and Uncle Tom enjoyed the Fair as much as we children, and we were not the only ones with powder and 'ticklers'. It was expected of my father to win a coconut and he would throw, whatever the cost, until he gained one. Later, as the years passed, I was pretty skilled myself at knocking the nuts out of the cups, but as a boy I was not silly enough to waste good money on such a gamble, as I noticed the base of each nut was packed in sawdust and pretty securely anchored in the cup.

Each year we went on the latest and most sophisticated roundabouts, and spent our 'fairings' on the fascinating sideshows: snakes, fat ladies, tattooed ladies, belly dancers, trained fleas which walked tight-ropes and pulled minute carriages, conjurors, jugglers, animal acts and magic shows where women disappeared or were sawn in half, or put in a box into which swords were thrust. I recall one dart stall which exhibited fascinating prizes; it bore the words, 'The Lord helps those who help themselves but the Lord help anyone caught helping himself here.' The hot sausage stall had the attraction that occasionally the stall-holder would say, 'You can dip your bread in the fat, sonny'; but I was never lucky enough to have the offer extended to me —I was very small!

After the Fair some part of it went on to Witney—the small town noted for blanket manufacture—about eleven miles outside Oxford and my father and uncle followed up the pleasures of the Oxford Fair by jaunts to Witney. On a few occasions I was with the party but it was a 'bachelor' do and we had to keep away from our grown-up relations until it was time to go home.

Fairs, occasional circuses—the grandest being Lord John Sanger's—and Bostock and Wombwell's Menagerie were thrilling events. This menagerie came at regular intervals to Gloucester Green, where it set up a huge marquee. Gloucester Green—now a bus station—was then the cattle market, being one huge expanse of concrete with iron pens to secure the cattle. The market itself was of great interest to a small boy. The auctioneering of cattle was incomprehensible. There were mock auctions of fascinating canteens of cutlery, vases, fountain pens, all catchpenny, glittering items made specially for these tricksters, who were skilled in leading on the more simple country folk and getting them so confused that they bid for 'lots' they had already paid for in part or in whole.

After market days the whole area was washed down and disinfected and it made a good playground for many of us— particularly for hide-and-seek. The authorities have succeeded in getting this market moved outside the city centre, and in this instance, one finds it difficult to be critical; but the magic went when the cattle market went from Gloucester Green.

Cinemas became our great attraction as they were built. One of the best was 'George Street', and it was here I went regularly every Saturday afternoon, generally staying to see the performance all round again—price threepence. There

61

were better seats at sixpence. From time to time I missed a performance when, having tried in vain to run errands for a copper or two or to sell a few jars or bottles, I lacked the necessary money. The box office issued metal tickets which were used time and time again. Sometimes they missed collecting one and we would try to 'pinch in' with it on another occasion.

Here I saw the great serials: 'The Exploits of Elaine' or 'The Clutching Hand', with a cast headed by Pearl White as the heroine, or the greatest serial of all 'The Perils of Pauline'; Craig Kennedy, the detective, was played by Arnold Daly, whom I never heard of again, and Wu Fang by Edwin Arden. These were the great days of what is now accepted as 'classic' cinema. Here we saw the latest Chaplin films as they were issued, as well as Buster Keaton, Fatty Arbuckle and Laurel and Hardy. But the greatest film I remember, was the Griffiths epic, 'The Birth of a Nation'. All these films I saw as a young boy. Later I went to other cinemas, all known by the name of the street in which they were situated: Queen Street, Walton Street and, cheapest of all, Castle Street—children's matinees, entrance one penny with sometimes an orange thrown in. 'It was bedlam!' as my father would describe a noisy throng.

But it was at George Street cinema that I saw the best films. Queen Street was later renowned for a considerable period for its first-class cinema orchestra under the direction of Archie Paine, who wore a velvet coat and looked magnificent as he conducted with the limelight on him. This was a great refinement and Queen Street had a class and a presentation superior to other cinemas. Archie Paine and his orchestra were such a success that they gave Sunday concerts in Oxford's Town Hall.

It was in Queen Street cinema that I would, from time to time, see the Rev. W. A. Spooner. He it was who had the habit of transposing initial letters, to produce 'Spoonerisms'. At the cinema he would take his seat right in the front where there were usually rows of empty seats, and I was told he was puzzled by the fact that everyone sat at the back when there were such nice front seats available.

Among the Spoonerisms I recall are the announcement, 'We will now sing hymn number 175, Kingquering Kongs their tatles tike' (Conquering Kings their titles take), and the reply he once made, looking at a blancmange, to a hostess who asked what he would like: 'I would like some of the stink puff.' Spooner, whom I met but never knew, died in 1930 and left a wonderful legacy by adding a word to the English language and lots of laughs. One last Spoonerism—he is reported to have said, 'For real enjoyment give me a well boiled icycle.'

The old New Theatre (now demolished for a newer New Theatre) with its stone and wooden seats in the gallery, introduced me to the Gilbert and Sullivan operas, which came to Oxford almost annually for two weeks with a cast of famous performers: Sir Henry Lytton, Bertha Lewis, Darrell Fancourt. I think no 'Savoyards' can ever have equalled them, but my father, who saw the original casts, said 'They are not a patch on them.'

The new New theatre is today one of the finest in the country but it was on the stage of its predecessor that I saw 'Trilby' with Julia Neilson Terry and 'The Scarlet Pimpernel' with Fred Terry, her father, as well as most of the gay operettas of the time: 'The Belle of New York', 'The Arcadians', 'San Toy', 'Floradora', 'The Quaker Girl' and many others.

I wonder if those stage-folk ever realised that they gave us lasting thrills and such intense pleasure that we have remembered them vividly all our lives. It was so worthwhile queuing for two hours or so, often in the cold and wet, and paying the sixpenny entrance charge for these enchantments. Later in life I met many stars, including Charlie Chaplin, Gregory Peck, 'Shnozzle Durante', Mistinguette and others. But alas! I never met the lovely Marilyn Monroe, whom I specially adored, nor have I yet met Maria Callas, who I think is the most fascinating woman in the world as well as a great singer and actress.

We ate hot meat-pies in the theatre gallery in the intervals; their savoury, mouth-watering smell and taste is with me yet! But I cannot remember if salesgirls brought them round. Though I think they did, we may have popped out to a nearby pie-shop in the interval.

One needed very little money to live a full and exciting life in Oxford; the very fact that we had to spend our pennies wisely made us all the more appreciative of the pleasures they bought. Of course, we were lucky in many ways. For instance, the best theatre companies came to Oxford with the stars of the period, and when I visited my cousin at Crewe and Nantwich, with touring companies appearing in their theatres, I realised their inferiority and our good fortune.

It is a mistake not to be born in Oxford, not only for the joys I have mentioned but also for the charm of the villages and particularly of the waterside pubs. Today, as in the past, they occupy an important place in the lives and indeed in the hearts of all Oxonians. What charm there is, what romance even in the names. There is, for example, the Rose Revived at Newbridge, with its sign of a rose in a mug of beer. Here in my teens we had the top of a loaf, a bowl of tomatoes and as much cheese and butter as we could eat for sixpence; but my father would often tell us of the days when he walked out into the country for a day and made his lunch off a few pints of beer and bread and cheese, butter and pickles. Then he bought an ounce of tobacco and drank several more pints on the way home and still he had change in his pocket from a half-crown he had started out with.

At Cumnor there is The Bear and Ragged Staff, and in this village how thrilled I was and in what awe I truly stood when, in the church, I gazed for the first time on what I had read about in history and romances—a real 'chained Bible'. It is a black letter Bible of 1611. I am still thrilled to see it although I have since handled the first Bibles to be printed with moveable type, which are incredibly rare and valuable.

All around these pubs is romance and history. It was at

A 'Stickyback' photograph of Tommy Joy, aged eleven (Stickybacks were a forerunner of Polyfoto)

My first drive in our Singer car with mother beside me and my youngest sister in the dicky seat

With my wife (extreme right) and friends on the ponies described in our Killarney escapade

Father as we remember him (front left)—on an outing . . .

Cumnor that the beautiful Amy Robsart (1532-1560) lived a secluded life in Cumnor Place. She met her death, we were taught, at the hands of Robert Dudley, though it could have been an accident. Dudley had become a favourite of Queen Elizabeth and it appears his wife, Amy, was in the way. She was found dead at the bottom of a staircase. Here is a real-life murder(?)mystery.

Only a few miles away is The Perch in the middle of Binsey Green, an old pub with a skittle alley on the lawn. I recall that there once was an old sloping wooden trough, to facilitate the return of the balls. The pub itself has the same charm today as it had for me when, on a spring evening, my mother and father and all of us children would walk there and play on the swings and be fascinated by the secluded arbours of living hedge, in the centre of each of which was a rough table and seats. There were then—and still are—pigeons in the dovecote and hundreds of swallows in the eaves of the old thatched roof.

Binsey Green or Binsey 'Treacle Mines'—for such it was called by the locals as a joke, probably based on the fact that the green can be very marshy, resembling black treacle—and the old Perch are as popular as ever, indeed more popular, as the motor car has made them more accessible to both undergraduates and townees.

There are a few, a very few, old cottages on Binsey Green, two quite lovely, and it is a dream of mine one day to live in one, but I think it is a dream which will never be realised, as I imagine the land and cottages belong to a college or the University authorities and go by some 'Grace and Favour' arrangement. No harm in that but, as Sam Goldwyn would have put it, 'that includes me out'.

Binsey has a particular nostalgic attraction for me; so deep that I am inclined to believe that I must have been associated with it in a past life. I go there often, making it something of a pilgrimage—following, as it happens, the true pilgrims of the Middle Ages, for this was once a holy shrine, with a miraculous well which could cure many ailments. The

'Wishing well', as we called it as children, is in the church-yard, which is reached by a rather long lane branching off on the left of Binsey Green. It is so remote that many people never see it and relatively few even know of its existence. All alone stands this tiny church, approached through a long avenue of magnificent chestnuts, and here in this avenue is the remains of a flood walk of stones which has always fascinated me, as I think of the pilgrims and parishioners who have walked them.

This flood-walk leads to the church, and it is there because this part is particularly low-lying and the way would frequently have been flooded. The legend connected with the holy well, which is in the churchyard, enclosed in a stone surround, is that a spring of water was 'called forth by St Margaret in answer to the prayers of St ffrediswyde'. St ffrediswyde is reputed to have built a chapel near the well, and it has been suggested that this at Binsey was the very beginning of anything at Oxford. The shrine soon became famous far and wide as a place of pilgrimage, so much so that there is a tradition of a town which sprang up to serve the multitudes who came to drink and bathe in the holy waters. The town was called Seckworth, but if it ever existed there is little—in fact, no—visible trace of it today. Royalty visited this holy place and the last royal pilgrims were King Henry VIII and Catherine of Aragon. These last two actually went for fertility reasons as Henry wanted a son. He would probably have done better to have gone to Willow Walk a shady lane which skirts Port Meadow. In my youth it was renowned for fertility 'rites' practised there.

If in America or Italy they had such a place as Binsey with its historic and religious associations, it would be a shrine to which millions of tourists would go; but at Oxford this beautiful, holy and romantic place is neglected and almost forgotten.

The most beautiful pub on the Thames is The Trout Inn at Godstow—a statement of fact, not a subject for debate. It is unspoiled today, unless the reader considers a place necesarily spoiled by popularity and crowds. I can remember The Trout when it was generally empty, as only a few locals and walkers and cyclists would visit it. But this wonderful old pub, dating back to the twelfth century, is really much the same today as it has been over the centuries. Its weir and madly rushing water, its school of large chub, some weighing well over 6 or 7lbs, which are plainly seen and almost feed from the hand on some clear days (lots of people mistake them for trout, but very few trout are there today), its peacocks in the grounds, its old, long rustic bridge (now unsafe) and the remains of Godstow Nunnery, are all as I remember them as a boy and as my father before me. Fair Rosamund (Clifford) lived at Godstow Nunnery across the water, built as far back as 1138. She was the acknowledged mistress of Henry II and it is possible she was poisoned, or murdered in some other way, by Henry's queen. So here is a second real-life murder mystery.

History, romance, so much beauty, so much life, no wonder the haunt has its devotees and always has had. My boyhood friend, Buzz Burrows, had his corner seat in The Trout and over very many years was always to be seen there. Buzz was the printer of *Isis*, the university magazine, since he had inherited a well-known local printing business. At one time he was also a quite famous *Daily Sketch* cartoonist, the 'Obstinate Artist'. Until his death just a year or two back Buzz was to be found at The Trout and literally hundreds of people looked forward as much to seeing Buzz as to the many other charms of the place, for he was a very charming man. We miss him as many of us miss the presence of the former owner of The Trout, Mrs Colman. She lived to a ripe old age, with her dog Bomber—so named because he apparently enjoyed being tossed into the madly rushing and boiling waters from the weir. 'Ma' Colman was a matriarchal character and her husband, who predeceased her by many years, could equally keep a young man in his place. In their day the draught Worthington was reckoned to be particularly potent and it was a regular trick to take someone there who was proud of his capacity to drink many pints without effect. The results were often spectacular.

So in these meadows, lanes and pubs one feels that almost every stone is a link with history, that everyone of importance has walked this way and enjoyed the lush countryside. And that indeed is not far from the truth. Only the local-born have the true feel of it all, but members of the university often come to love it with much the same devotion. They are, of course, being presumptuous but we tolerate their patronage of things which are 'ours' because we love the place. Town and gown have a long history of being at variance with each other, often leading to battles and bloodshed, but of course today the undergraduates are no longer called or looked upon as 'The Gentlemen'. In many ways it is a pity but the standards of dress, speech, behaviour, even food and drink, to say nothing of the service which college servants were once called upon to give and, in the main, took a pride in giving, have deteriorated, so much so that the locals no longer feel inferior but quite the reverse.

Be that as it may, people will always fall in love with Oxford, now and in centuries to come, and those who wander the lanes and meadows outside the city boundaries will find a unique treasure which they, like me, will ever cherish. I could go on reminiscing, about Oxford pubs until I had written a whole book about them—which may seem strange, as I hardly ever drank beer or spirits, but they are social places, more local clubs than bars. The Chequers at lovely-sounding Bablock Hythe is another pub not far from the others I have mentioned. The short way to it, until recent times, necessitated crossing the river by means of a 'car ferry'; more accurately it was first a horse and cart ferry and it was terrific fun to go across in this barge which was hauled by pulling on the thick hawser which was fixed across the river at about shoulder height. The ferry barge had wooden rollers to save wear on the rope.

We children were even allowed to pull on the rope and help propel the boat. Alas! the ferry is there no longer! The fare was a penny. One day I cycled there but, having no penny, remained standing forlornly on the bank. 'Do you want to come across, young Joy?' shouted the boatman. I explained the situation and asked how he knew my name. 'Oh!' he said, 'I know Alf Joy's bike, it's the only one I have seen like it.' On our way across—he knew by the way that my father would buy him a drink next time they met, for father was ever generous in this way—we examined my father's bike, which I was that day riding. I too, had never seen anything like it! Everything was curved, the bar which is usually straight on a man's bicycle was curved, so were all the wheel forks. It had not been buckled, it had been made that way. Anyway it served me in good stead that day and that was not the only time.

VI

An apprentice to a bookseller was a pretty low form of animal life, but even so, in our opinion we were superior to those not apprenticed, regarding ourselves as students rather than junior assistants. Over all, our seniors were the most kindly people imaginable but it is only in retrospect that one truly appreciates this.

Booksellers are, in literature, generally regarded with favour. Dr Johnson said, 'Booksellers are generous, liberal-minded men,' and so I have found them. They are, indeed, exceptionally nice people. It is a trade too which attracts and perhaps creates 'eccentrics'. A very pleasant man was our chief clerk at Thornton's. We called him 'Diddy' (I do not know why, as his real name was Sawyer). He was a gentle, lovable person, with a trick of palming coins so that they disappeared. We would go to the cash desk and call out, 'Three-and-six, five shillings.' This meant we were tendering five shillings for a three-and-sixpenny purchase and required one-and-six change. He would pretend to hand the money to you, even clicking the coins on the counter, but when you tried to pick them up they were not there.

He would sometimes greet one with, 'Pardon me, thou bleeding piece of earth,' from Shakespeare's 'Julius Caesar' or, apropos of nothing, 'If while walking in the garden I should kick you up the arse, would you greatly be offended if I said, please let me pass?' (I suspect this to be a parody of

70

something by Lewis Carroll.) Another of his greetings was 'Hail to thee blithe spirit' from 'To a skylark' by Shelley.

The office door was covered in small bullet holes because the staff had target practice when the boss was out. 'Diddy' was a good bowler at cricket and would throw a large piece of rubber at you as you walked up the long narrow shop. One day he did this at the precise moment when an assistant leaned out into the passage way, so that the rubber hit him hard and knocked him out for a moment or two. Our problem was to revive him before the boss returned.

F. S. Thornton was a disciplinarian, but a fine man and a great bookseller. Perhaps just because he was strict, we took advantage as soon as his back was turned. He went to the bank and was absent for about half an hour from ten-thirty until eleven o'clock in the morning. All the staff then disappeared to make a cup of Oxo. They did not have coffee, as the milk and sugar complicated things and there was of course, no such thing as instant coffee, but I remember there was bottled Camp coffee, which could be made by simply pouring hot water on the thick liquid.

Most of the staff bought an Oxo cube, particularly in winter, for the shop was cold and draughty. There was an old coke tortoise-stove in the basement on which was a bucket and this together with one roller-towel a week were more or less the sum of toilet arrangements. The bucket of water heated on the stove became thick with scum as assistants washed their hands in it. The alternative was the cold tap. Conditions generally were a bit Dickensian, and we were all living on low wages. Experienced assistants, married men, were lucky if they received much above two pounds per week. The business could not afford more and for many weeks in vacations there were practically no customers, but the post orders from all over the world helped to keep things going. To be absolutely just, two pounds a week was about the average wage for a sales assistant in any form of retailing.

Thorntons had, and still has, a large postal trade, and they also supplied books for the boys at Oxford High School, the school which T. E. Lawrence attended. He was just before my time, and as far as I know, I never served him, although in later years I knew many of his more intimate friends, including John Snow, his legal adviser.

This selling of books to schools in which there was little profit was augmented by the more profitable selling of second-hand books to universities all over the world, and in term-time particularly, to members of Oxford University.

When few customers were in the shop, the staff, numbering a dozen or so, was occupied in mail-order work—looking out the books ordered through the post—in ordering those titles not in stock from the publishers, in placing new stock in its correct position on the shelves and in compiling cata-logues.

My first job was to register the post, which meant giving each letter a number and entering the name and address of the customer against the number in the Letter Book. After-wards, among other jobs, I licked the small sticky labels, giving the name and address of the firm, that were affixed inside each book before it was placed on the shelves.

Later—much later—I was competent to value and to enter in code the cost price in each book and to mark the selling price. We worked on a small trading margin and many books purchased remained on the shelves for years before they were sold and, of course, several never sold at all. I truly think it possible that a few books which I purchased as far back as 1930 are still there on the shelves. By living with books day after day, by research into catalogues, one gradually acquired a sound knowledge of books both new and second-hand, and by following the business system which had evolved for over a century I started to learn, too, to be a good business man. All this served me in good stead in the years to come, as I have detailed in my first book, *Bookselling*, which was published by Pitman in 1952. This became the first official textbook of the trade. It is not, I feel, very much my book; I merely set down for the first time those things I had been taught so well by Mr F. S. Thornton.

Thornton's specialised in Theology and Greek and Latin Classics, but I became particularly interested in Oriental and Semitic books—so much so that I started their Oriental section, and built it up to such a degree that soon we were selling these categories of books to universities and individuals all over the world. It is pleasing to know that the Oriental department is today a most important part of the business in this shop where I served my apprenticeship.

As years passed, largely as a result of my writing articles for the *Publishers Circular* and *The Bookseller* and having lectured on the book trade and taught in evening classes, I gained something of a reputation and was in a very small way regarded as a 'success'.

Mr Schollick, a Director of Blackwell's, tells the story—apocryphal, I am sure—but gratifying, of how when he was showing a group of booksellers round Oxford, he paused in the middle of Broad Street to show them the cross marked in the middle of the road where a charred stake was found and where, it is believed, one of the martyrs—Ridley, Latimer or Cranmer—was burned on this spot. He says they showed little interest but when he observed that the shop opposite was where Tommy Joy served his apprenticeship, they came to life immediately and were thrilled to see this 'historic landmark'!

Blackwell's, Parker's and Thornton's were the leading Oxford booksellers and frequently all three would be called upon to offer for a library or collection of books. It is an amazing fact that the 'valuations' were usually identical, or within a few shillings of each other, which proves that the buyers—and in due course I became one of the leading ones in Oxford—knew their business.

Books under beds, sometimes with an occupant too lazy to get up, books on the tops of kitchen ranges, in kitchen ovens, books in cellars, attics, outhouses, whole libraries and small collections of a dozen or so ranging from *The Morphology of Angiosperms* to Fielding's *Tom Jones*, or *Eric, or Little by Little*, all came our way. We could value (and some of us, indeed, were licensed valuers in those days) medical, technical, mathematical, belles lettres, history, classics in any language, first editions, private press books, in fact almost any book on any subject. We knew our classics from Aristotle to Xenophon—yes, every text, every 'crib', every publisher, every price.

Oxford was a wonderful experience and a first-class training ground for a bookseller and I was lucky in my firm and in my boss. I dedicated my book *Bookselling* to Mr F. S. Thornton out of gratitude and affectionate regard. He lived to the ripe age of ninety. F. S. Thornton is particularly remembered in the British book trade for his early interest and pioneer work in the education of booksellers' assistants. He was of the highest integrity and so honest in his dealings that it must have sometimes been difficult to run the business at a profit. He himself worked almost to the day he died and worked as hard as any member of the staff. He was not very approachable—probably a shy man—and most of us stood a little in awe of him. I know I did and, as we met from time to time over many years, I never quite lost that feeling; but I, too, am a little shy. One day I felt it necessary to confess this to a Lady-in-Waiting for whom I had arranged to have an autographing session in the Stores in London of her book on a member of the Royal Household. 'I noticed it, Mr Joy,' she said, 'but then, all nice people are a little shy.' I was greatly comforted by this.

One day, in my apprenticeship years at Thornton's, the boss went off a little early and I threw a Macmillan's Elementary Classic, quite a small book, at one of the assistants. Quick as a flash he was on the other side of the glass door and the book, to my horror, sailed clean through it! I had to confess next morning. 'Was it an accident?' asked Mr Thornton. My chorister training had made me a George Washington—whatever the consequences, we did not lie—and so I replied, 'No, sir—not really.' 'Well, you cannot expect me to pay for your fooling about,' he said, 'and I will deduct the cost from your wages.' But he never did and, although I was appreciative, I could not pluck up the courage to thank him.

One of the most interesting libraries we bought at Thornton's was that of the Rev. Canon Dalton, Dean of Windsor and tutor to members of the Royal Family. I felt very important as we went into Windsor Castle, even as I do today when I occasionally go through the gates of Buckingham Palace in a taxi to make a special delivery of books.

Mr Thornton and I went to Windsor to value and get the books ready for transportation by van to Oxford. This was an unusual collection of books, predominantly theological, but it included a number of beautiful books in fine presentation bindings containing inscriptions and signatures of members of the Royal Family over many years. They would fetch enormous prices today but we sold them for what appeared to be a fair price at the time.

Canon Dalton had a habit of using his correspondence to mark places in the books he was reading and we were asked to return any letters we found. The correspondence was voluminous and most interesting, including letters from Queen Victoria regarding the progress and education of the family. All letters were returned, of course, as promised.

In this Dalton library I made an interesting discovery of unique folio volumes of half-plate photographs. These were the originals taken on the cruise of the *Bacchante*, the voyage on which were the two princes, H.R.H. The Duke of Clarence and H.R.H. Prince George. The bindings were broken and there was nothing to indicate whether the photographs were important or not, but by research and with reference to the books written about the voyage, I was able to identify them, and Mr Thornton agreed that we should present them to the library at Windsor Castle. This was done, and we proudly exhibited the letter of thanks, headed Windsor Castle, in the shop window.

I was no angel and often up to mischief but usually careful not to be caught. I had learnt a little ju-jitsu at the Y.M.C.A., where five Japanese experts—the first in this

75

country I believe, who were here to train members of the university—gave us lessons and I tended to use my 'expertise' on my colleagues.

One day one of the senior assistants named Rowell, who was a great pal of mine, was, as I thought, bending over to reach a book on one of the lower shelves. I at once caught hold of him and threw him to one side. To my horror it was a customer. I can still see the look on his face! I just panicked and got out of the room as quickly as possible.

The Oxford Y.M.C.A. in George Street was a splendid organisation. It kept us out of the pubs and added to our opportunities in sports and games; and here I learned to debate. The debating society was so good that it was able to take on members of the Oxford Union and acquit itself well. Every week the debating hall was full. Once a year we had a mock trial, which was conducted on serious lines although the characters were eccentric and the costumes bizarre. I remember one impressive 'witness' gave her name as 'Nurse Epsom'. 'Undoubtedly one of our best workers,' said the learned counsel.

In the course of time I could make a reasonable speech and this served me in good stead in the years to come. I also learned to play chess, draughts and bridge, and coxed the crew. Coxing an eight on the Isis is an exciting experience and our annual bumping races are treasured memories. We had access to certain of the college barges stationed on the shore of Christ Church meadows. On one regatta day, feeling rather proud and important, I ferried a party of people, including my father, from the tow-path to the barge. I got them over safely and then stood at one end of the ferry punt, holding it with the pole while a race passed. I was smartly attired in flannels, blazer and my cox's cap. Then I took a step back straight into the water and had to swim for it. The blue of my blazer ran into my white flannels, my cap floated downstream and my father laughed loudly with the large crowd, as I was ignominiously pulled on to the barge. I felt terrible and looked it, as in borrowed togs I prepared for the next race—which we lost! Certainly this was one of the most embarrassing moments of my life.

Still, that was not as funny as when my aunt fell down a coal-hole! She was pushing a perambulator along an Oxford street and walked on one of those circular iron plates on the pavement. The plate gave way and my aunt, who is a little thing, disappeared down the hole, and the perambulator with the child continued on its way. Since she was not badly hurt and the child was saved by a passing pedestrian, the family saw more humour than pathos in the situation!

The great event of our rowing season was the week of the Bumping Races. The boats (there are about twelve or thirteen altogether) are staked out so that at the start there is the same amount of space between each boat. The starting gun is fired and the object of each crew is to breach the gap and 'bump' the boat in front. If a crew succeeds in doing this they take the place of the 'bumped' crew on the following day and thus have moved up one place. In course of time a crew can thus become 'Head of the River'.

After the races, the crews who have been 'in training'— no smoking, drinking, or girls—go out on the spree. I joined in the revels after the racing and was quickly tipsy on a glass or two of strong ale. Bawdy 'Togger' songs are sung— absolutely disgusting! and wonderful fun for the adolescent. I give two verses which convey the general idea:

I wish I had a thousand bricks to build our
    chimney higher
To stop the neighbours' cats from piddling
    on our fire.

Chorus:
    There is rest, there is rest
    In my father's house there is rest.

I wish I was a diamond brooch upon my true
    love's breast,

As every time she heaved a sigh, I'd see the
cuckoo's nest.

Chorus:
> There is rest, there is rest
> In my father's house there is rest.

VII

It takes many years of practical experience to become an efficient and knowledgeable bookseller and the general public has little comprehension of what is involved. Over the years I have interviewed literally thousands of people who would like to work in a bookshop, which they regard as a clean, pleasant, genteel occupation. On being asked why they want to become booksellers they almost invariably reply, 'Because I love books.' One bookseller I know would reply crushingly, 'I love money but that does not qualify me to become Chancellor of the Exchequer.'

The love of books and a good education are not enough. True, these are necessary requirements, as are honesty, integrity, business ability, industry and so on. But what is chiefly required is experience, which can only be obtained by years of practical bookselling, during which time one must learn the contents of reference books, authors, titles (remember around 35,000 new books are published each year, and over one quarter of a million titles are in print at one time in Great Britain alone). One must know publishers, prices and classifications—and not only of books in print but of books published in past years. A photographic memory and a real, sustained interest over the years makes a bookseller.

When I entered the trade there were no textbooks on bookselling available and there was a great need for one, as the education and training of assistants to study for the newly instituted Diploma in Bookselling became increasingly important. So in due course I wrote one called *Bookselling*, which Pitman's published in 1952. I had taken the first courses arranged by the Booksellers Association and passed the examination, thus becoming a 'qualified bookseller by examination'. At this stage I thought I knew it all but after fifty years I am still learning. A further ten years passed before I felt qualified to lecture on various aspects of bookselling, ultimately being elected Chairman of the Education Board.

Just before I left Oxford to work in London, I was honoured by being elected Chairman of the Oxford Booksellers and Assistants Association, though it was in fact by no means an important post. One year a local master bookseller was Chairman and the next year an assistant was elected. One of those enlightened, stimulating ideas one associates with Oxford bookselling.

This Association had all kinds of meetings in Blackwell's. In particular we listened to poetry readings by John Masefield, a treasured memory, and to Bob Rowles singing sea shanties, a memory equally treasured by many of us. We played cricket against Cambridge booksellers and we also played a team at Warneford Asylum. I was no good at cricket but sometimes kept the score. The trouble at Warneford Asylum was the difficulty in knowing the staff from the inmates. On one occasion a man scoring with me said, 'Have you got a wireless set?' I replied, 'No.' 'We have,' he said. He continued to ask questions, 'Have you got this, have you got that?' Finally he said, 'If you would be advised by me, you should try to get in here quickly, because the place is filling up and it will be more difficult later.' At tea I noticed he took two slices of bread and butter and slipped a piece of cake between them! Pathetic, of course, but it is human to see the funny side. I suppose on some previous occasion the poor fellow had found there was no cake left when he had eaten his bread and butter, and his anxiety complex gave him concern for both my future welfare and his meal.

My text-book *Bookselling* sold out, so I re-wrote and expanded the whole book, which was again published by Pitman in 1964 as *The Truth about Bookselling*, a title based on Sir Stanley Unwin's classic, *The Truth about Publishing*. I hoped my book would be a kind of companion volume to Sir Stanley's and, with characterisic generosity, Sir Stanley wrote a Foreword for my book and by so doing sanctioned, as it were, my adaptation of his title.

I was lucky in having had a more varied experience than many of my colleagues and this experience of big business, coupled with my years as a bookseller, perhaps qualified me to write with more detachment than I would have done as a bookseller only; for, as the following pages will show, after leaving Oxford I had a wide experience in business in the departmental store world.

First I became Manager of Harrods Library. This was a very important appointment indeed—one of the plum jobs of the book trade; so much so that I was regarded as a success, by some almost a 'Dick Whittington'. Harrods have the largest circulating library in the country, which I managed, and later I was also appointed Manager of the Book Department, again the largest in any departmental store in the country and, in my view, the best in the world.

After a period of ten very happy and successful years at Harrods, I left to take up an appointment at the Army & Navy Stores in Westminster as Head Book Buyer and there I founded the circulating library, which still flourishes. I was promoted to Merchandise Manager and finally, until my retirement from the stores, to Deputy Managing Director. I shall tell more of all this later on, but it was these experiences, together with the fact that I had served from youth on almost every committee of the Booksellers Association, that enabled me to write *The Truth about Bookselling*.

But to return to this business of bookselling. 'How do you know how many books to buy?' people often ask me. 'You cannot read them all.' This is a difficult question to answer because one never knows how much is 'flair' and how much is knowledge based on experience. I suppose it is a mixture of both.

As I have said, around 35,000 new titles are published in Great Britain every year or say one hundred every working day. Obviously this presents a problem, but probably over half of these books can be ruled out as far as buying for stock is concerned, because they are Government publications or technical, scientific or medical books which are not usually stocked unless the business specialises in one or more of these subjects. Even so, no other trade has the equivalent of one hundred new 'lines' every day and a bookseller is expected to anticipate the exact demand for each title to meet customers' requirements. The buying of books for stock is a most absorbing occupation and a most exasperating one, yet one never tires of it.

The publishers' representatives are a great help and every bookseller acknowledges indebtedness to them. They do not read all the books they subscribe to a bookseller, but they are knowledgeable about the selling potential of a book. Some of them are so good and trustworthy that you could, with confidence, give them your order book and allow them to fill in the titles and numbers of copies, as over the years they get to know the individual requirements of each bookshop on which they call.

Of course, no bookseller is competent to judge all the books on special subjects that pass through his hands and therefore to read many of them would be rather a waste of time. But booksellers lucky enough to be quick, retentive readers, who can judge the style and merit of a book, even though the subject is unfamiliar, who possess a memory for past achievements and literary standing of certain authors—these have the assets necessary for both book-buying and bookselling.

Above all, a good bookseller needs insatiable mental curiosity and wide interests, a knowledge and love of literature, and a tolerant, unbiased attitude to politics, religion and new trends. Finally, and most important, he must love people.

VIII

I often say there is no such thing as bad staff, there are only bad managers, and throughout my career I have been blessed with wonderful staff. I fume when I read criticism in the press of the inadequacy of shop assistants, who, the writers say, 'could not care less'. Such articles are often written by unimaginative and sensation-seeking reporters. The truth is that shop assistants generally, in my experience, do their best and *do* care, but much is required of them and they cannot all have the knowledge the public expects. We must have beginners and, of course, we can all make mistakes.

Even the perfect secretary can make a mistake and one of mine once ended a letter to a difficult customer, 'Wishing you the *complaints* of the season'! Staff are fun and one never knows what will happen next.

Miss Christina Foyle tells the story of a particularly attractive female assistant, whom they placed in their theological department; she was constantly warding off sex-starved clerics. One day, when she was sorting out books on the high shelves so that she was showing a lot of leg, a 'reverend gentleman' chased her up a ladder. She was then heard to exclaim, 'Who do you think I am? Maria Monk?'

One of my assistants reported that she had seen a customer steal a book and put it in his pocket. The supervisor said, 'Are you quite sure?' 'Oh, absolutely,' she replied. 'I did not know what to do, so I pushed past him, took it out and put it back into stock.' I do not recommend this method of dealing with a book thief but it showed initiative.

Book thieves are a terrible nuisance and must be stopped, because one encourages others. Thieving was so prevalent in one shop that young people came in regularly to steal with a view to selling the books to other booksellers. One young man, on being caught, said he and his friends did it regularly to get money to buy their lunch. 'We call them Literary Luncheons,' he said.

I can often spot a book thief because he does not behave normally. 'That man, I think, will steal a book,' I may say to one of the staff and, when he is caught doing so, they express surprise that I knew in advance. Like Sherlock Holmes, I am loath to explain how I knew as I remember that when Holmes explained his method of deduction to Dr Watson, the latter commented 'How absurdly simple.' It is simple when you know how! For example, all the customers are browsing with their heads down, or their attention focussed on the shelves, but the potential book thief keeps looking around. He often wears a raincoat into the inside pocket of which he can easily slip books and, of course, if he is holding a carrier bag, or any kind of case into which books can easily be slipped, he is doubly suspect.

One of the most curious cases I experienced was at Oxford, where I found some forty or fifty books, some quite expensive, lying flat on the top of the bookshelves in one of the upstairs rooms. The books, on a variety of subjects, were not from our stock—a fact that was obvious since, firstly, the room was devoted entirely to theological works. And secondly, all books we bought carried our code mark. So there was no doubt these books had not just been wrongly sorted by a junior. I removed the books and a few days later another lot appeared, and so it went on for months. I suspected someone was arriving with a bag of books and exchanging them for others from our stock, but no stock appeared to be missing. Ultimately we caught the man responsible and asked for an explanation. He said he had been left a property that included a large collection of books and, not knowing how to get rid of them, he brought them along, a caseful at a time, and dumped them on us. I believed his story, strange as it was, but we would willingly have taken all the books off his hands and paid him for them. Having long ago dispersed the collection, we had no idea of the total value and could not pay him, but he was not interested in payment.

Thieves, cranks and 'characters' are all part of a book-seller's life. Bookselling is certainly, of all trades, the one in which it is not necessary to be crazy oneself—but it helps!

Bookselling attracts society girls and, contrary to general opinion, 'pin-money' girls are, in my experience, by and large hard-working and painstaking, and loved by staff and customer alike. They set a splendid example and live up to 'noblesse oblige', to a marked degree. Willing, capable, industrious, they are a credit to their upbringing and not at all spoiled by affluence or rank. I attended the wedding of one recently in the Guards Chapel and it was an impressive occasion. Several of my staff were present and one of them actually made the bridesmaids' dresses. So popular was this girl that even the doorman at Fortnum & Mason's sent a telegram of congratulation.

As I grow older I feel privileged to be with the modern generation. Their approach to life may be rather shattering but I find them conscientious, hardworking, loyal and lively to be with. This modern generation is frank and outspoken, and not afraid to express an opinion, whereas we were timid, kept in our place, the victims of 'children should be seen and not heard' and that sort of nonsense. I know which *I* prefer, and at no time has young staff been more competent, more energetic (something to do with good food?) and more willing.

Management must be skilled, courteous, kind and under-standing—but *never weak*—or there will be trouble. There are too many old-fashioned managers who, living in the past, simply cannot cope with staff today. Overall it simply boils down to leadership and loving people. If you do not love people you cannot manage them. One's staff must be like a large family, each individual has strengths and weaknesses, and these must be recognised and understood, but one should never lightly dismiss people because of limitations and failings.

The art of management is to help and encourage; to place square pegs into square holes and thus to ensure that there is a place and prosperity for everyone. Sometimes this appears to be a thankless task; there are disappointments. But over the years staff look to a just, kind manager as a father figure and in time come to him with their troubles. This is not only rewarding in itself but, from a business point of view, it spells success indeed. Blessed with good loyal staff, business life is a pleasure and a profitable one at that. It is much easier to be popular than to be respected but popularity frequently is achieved by weak management and weak management is bad management. Kindness, courtesy and justice are essential in dealing with staff despite the fact that kindness can and will be mistaken for weakness, courtesy for artfulness and justice for favouritism, but a person of high integrity will gain respect and over the years may ultimately succeed in obtaining the rare goal of respect and a measure of popularity at one and the same time.

When I finished my apprenticeship I came to London and obtained a position, first with a George Salby, an Oriental bookseller in Little Russell Street by the British Museum and later as manager of the mail order section of Denny's in the Strand. Denny's was quite a famous bookshop, selling new books only, but now, like a number of other good bookshops, it has also gone, although the firm is still in existence in the City.

This was the year of the General Strike and one remembers the buses being driven by volunteers, the drivers being protected by wire mesh round the front of the bus. A ride on the tube with volunteer drivers of the trains could be rather alarming. Once I remember getting a lift on a coal cart with a few others but we were pulled off by a crowd of strikers in Camden Town. I walked to and from Highgate daily from the Strand and in those days our only anxiety was to get to work and keep the business running.

Today a great change has taken place and not only students, but perhaps their tutors too, would support the strikers, putting the welfare of the country last, the individual's first. I feel our generation had better priorities. We must all be grateful that there is now less poverty, more employment and much better working conditions; but, though I, for one, would not wish to return to 'the good old days', I sometimes wonder if there is as much true happiness today? I see too much evidence of discontent, too many layabouts. The bright spot for me is in the workers I meet in the literary world— they do a grand job and are happy.

Life was not all that bad in London on a small wage. You could buy a three-course luncheon at Slaters, quite a good class restaurant, for one shilling and sixpence. Of course, wages were low and at three pounds per week at Denny's I was considered well paid. My digs in Highgate cost twenty-five shillings per week including breakfast and an evening meal. As long as one had regular work one was comparatively well off, but if misfortune struck—accident, prolonged sickness or unemployment—the situation could be serious. Fortunately I have never known a good bookseller unemployed for long. There are all too few of them.

My old boss, F. S. Thornton, wanted me back and offered me what was then a high wage for Oxford, three pounds ten shillings per week, as head cataloguer and buyer, and I returned to Oxford very happy to be home again. I married in 1932 and my salary was raised to three pounds fifteen shillings per week. I gave my wife one pound five shillings for housekeeping, including light and fuel. We managed comfortably and had a holiday away each year. People find it difficult to believe we managed on so little but many managed on less around 1930—rent was less than £1 per week. The average weekly wage, I should say, was about two pounds ten shillings. In those days there was little or no inflation. A pound was worth a pound year after year, so you could budget

88

and save, knowing just where you were. Only a small amount was deducted from wages for National Health. Income Tax was low—there was none on small salaries—and there were no Pay As You Earn deductions.

Now, for some years, I bought and sold books, cycling out to the more distant parts of Oxford to see collections that people wished to sell. In the vacations I compiled catalogues of Greek and Latin classics, rare books and first editions. The limited edition craze was going on at this time and ended with the American Wall Street collapse (1929). Many people had been buying the books of the Nonesuch Press, Golden Cockerel Press, and older presses like Ashendene, speculatively, and the market was flooded as soon as the speculators tried to sell. There is now something of a revival in the collection of limited editions and private press books, doubtless in some measure due to the increased number of libraries in the world all eager to build up their collections.

Most of those presses which had produced fine limited editions ceased production; this was a pity as they published good work, using beautiful type on excellent paper, often with splendid illustrations and attractive bindings. Today the prices are very much higher than the original published prices for almost all of them. The market for the modern first edition also collapsed at the time of the Wall Street crash, but those who did not panic and kept their books have done well. Over the years book prices have gone up, they always have and they always will. The secret is to buy the best—the best authors, the best editions and the finest copies and hold on to them for ten years or more. Thus you can enjoy their possession and one day sell them at a profit.

The true book collector buys because he wants the book. He wants to possess good editions with fine illustrations and luxury bindings. He is not unconscious of the fact that they may increase in value but he is not primarily motivated by this possibility.

The exciting thing about second-hand book-buying is the knowledge that the world is still full of 'lost treasures' and you never know when one is coming your way. When one makes an offer, it is usually a fair one, but one is in something of a quandary from time to time because though the seller may consider he has just a number of rubbishy old books to dispose of, the bookseller spots one or two that are valuable. If he discloses this fact, time after time he loses the chance to buy, as the owner will say something to the effect that he did not appreciate any were of value and he would like to think about it.

On several occasions I have disclosed to the owners the true value, only to find the books being subsequently offered for sale at one of the big book auctions. Once this was particularly annoying, as I wanted a certain book for the Bodleian Library which was without a copy. I offered the customer the full amount that the Library would pay, which meant no profit at all for my firm, but the customer put it into the auction room. Yet if I had not been honest about its value, he would have sold it to me for a few shillings.

IX

What motivates one? Ambition? Excitement? The struggle against frustration? The desire to express oneself more fully in one's work, to extend oneself? Some combination of all of these, perhaps, motivated me to change from a safe and comfortable life in Oxford. I had married, and my wife and I had a nice new flat in St John's Road, within easy walking distance of the shop in the Broad where I worked. I had a good and interesting position but I was restless and something within me drove me to try London once again. I felt I could do better and I wanted to work in a larger organisation with more prospects.

My wife was a first-class secretary, having trained and worked at Wolsey Hall, the world-famous correspondence college, so together we felt secure, although I preferred that it should not be necessary for her to work full time.

A post was advertised in Harrods Library, for which I applied, and I was appointed senior assistant there. Cadness Page was Head Librarian and the Hon. Andrew Shirley was his deputy, I started as third-in-command, in charge of the sale of the ex-library books. This was a large department and my post carried with it seniority rank—rather like being a first lieutenant.

To go from an Oxford bookshop with a staff of about a dozen people to one of the largest and best departmental stores in the world, with a staff of around six thousand, was exciting, terrifying, amusing and the beginning of a breakthrough financially—the few pounds a week I had been earning becoming something closer, shall we say, to the salary of a Cabinet Minister. The surprising thing life has taught me is that, given the opportunity and experience, almost all human beings can accomplish very much more than they deem themselves capable of.

I was lucky in my career from the beginning in having people above me whom I respected, people who themselves were hard-working and capable, of high integrity and interested in my progress and welfare.

The head of Harrods, then Sir Woodman Burbidge and, later, his son, Sir Richard, were the 'merchant princes' of their age: loved and respected by their huge staff, and throughout the business world, as, indeed, are their successors at Harrods.

Whatever has happened to so much big business over the last two decades? Mergers and American methods have brought evils with them. The unscrupulous Smart Alec seems now to be much admired. High ethical standards are apt to be regarded as 'old-fashioned ideals'. Big business is now admitted to be a rat race. I suppose that is all right for rats, since perhaps they can enjoy the fight for survival—but I, thank God, have lived largely in a more gracious age in business, when old staff, not only old senior staff, were looked after and had a special, honourable place in the firm. Their past services were remembered and appreciated. In my day van men and porters would be known by their Christian names to the top executives, who truly regarded them as being every bit as valuable, in their own way, to the firm as those in higher positions, as indeed they were. Of course, much of this still exists but it appears to be dying with my generation.

Harrods's van men were, and still are, a remarkable body of men. They will get goods delivered in spite of snow, ice, breakdowns and the usual hazards of the roads. The spirit of Harrods was one of service throughout the store. I was fascinated and exhilarated by it. Within a week I loved

Harrods and I still do. My ten years there were happy years.

First I managed the library only, with a staff of around one hundred and later, as I have already said, I managed the book department in addition to the library. I was lucky and succeeded in doubling the large turnover of the book department.

A departmental store is a world in itself, full of humorous incidents and not without tragedy, for, working with a large body of people, one knows and is interested in the everyday happenings of their lives.

On my arrival at Harrods I benefited from the staff training classes where, besides learning the history and tradition of the firm as well as the 'system', one had the opportunity of making friends in the classroom. One would often recognise fellow 'trainees' at coffee—and other—breaks and could join them. So I was never lonely from my first days at Harrods.

Working at Harrods was fun: we had a wonderful sports ground, a theatre for amateur dramatics and staff dances. It was also a great business opportunity for me and the beginning, although I did not know it then, of my top management training. My Oxford experience served me in good stead and I had a wider and, over all, better knowledge of the trade than most at my age.

It was fun to be working with so many absolutely stunning women! I have always been a feminist and early recognised, as I have mentioned, that women are physically much stronger than is generally imagined and just as well equipped mentally. They are extremely conscientious and loyal. After years of management of thousands of women, my conclusions regarding them are the same as those I formed in my early years of management in Harrods, and any success I have had has been largely due to 'the women in my life'.

There are a few cardinal rules in running a successful business and some of them appear in various places in this book, but these rules for success are as difficult as the Ten Commandments to observe. As years roll on, I find the richest reward for a businessman is to be held in affectionate regard by his colleagues and members of the staff. A few of my original staff are still active in Harrods library and book department and, of course, many I worked with are still at the Army & Navy Stores. It means a lot to have a sincere, warm welcome when I revisit them.

Good management is largely a matter of guts and commonsense. One must endeavour to do the right thing for the welfare of the firm and for all employees. The greatest failing of managers is often a lack of moral courage. It is often vital for those in authority to fight for those things they believe to be right, even at the expense of their individual welfare. The chairman and board of directors may not exactly love you when you find it necessary to advise measures contrary to their wishes, but they won't hate you either for speaking out. Let us admit that from time to time 'fighters' have lost their jobs, but not if they went about things in the proper manner in a good company with a sound chairman. The character of the chairman sets the tone of any company. If he is a man of lofty principles, utterly sound and reliable, then no one under him need fear if they are conscientiously doing their jobs. Top executives always protest they do not want 'yes-men', but some fool themselves, as they really resent the expressions of opinion which differ from their own. Yet, I believe many more managers ultimately fail because they would rather take the easy way than the more difficult one they know to be right. To succeed one must always be polite and diplomatic, but a 'yes-man' is unlikely to reach the top and still less likely to stay there. In spite of the obvious risks it is the men of courage and determination who tend to succeed. I was slowly learning these things as I progressed in the departmental store.

Harrods is regarded by many as the 'university' of the departmental store world and wherever one goes one finds, at the top, people who trained at Harrods. I believe it was the making of me, as gradually I changed from bookman to a business man with a specialised knowledge of the book trade.

Customers have interesting foibles and in the library it was not uncommon for wealthy ladies to ask, and express willingness to pay extra, to borrow each time absolutely new books, because they were afraid of contamination from a book which had been in other hands. I wondered if they felt the same way about paper money! But there is really no evidence to support these exaggerated fears. Cashiers and librarians enjoy pretty average health! In any case, books in the course of manufacture are continually touched by hand.

I did install in the children's library a sterilising cabinet into which all books were placed on their return. The purpose was to satisfy parents that the usual children's illnesses would not be contracted through the circulation of library books. It may have been effective, but I never had much faith in it. Nevertheless it was a good advertising gimmick and if it only gave parents peace of mind, I suppose it was worth while and the smell was pleasant!

Readers would, from time to time, complain if they found the subject of a book 'disgusting' and ask me to remove it from the library shelves, or would threaten to close their accounts if I continued to circulate it. As for these self-appointed censors—'A pox on them!' Of course, if we refused to sell or stock any title for any reason, we were again in trouble, being accused of religious or political bias or of being stupid old fuddy-duddy moralists. If a book was banned and we had to recall copies that were out on loan from the library, surprisingly the books were either 'dropped in the bath and ruined', or more commonly, 'the dog chewed it up!' (Extraordinary, the way dogs suddenly became selective in their taste for literature!)

I acquired something of a reputation for knowledge of the law regarding so-called 'obscene publications'; particularly with the well-known publisher, Walter Hutchinson. He so valued my opinion that he would consult me sometimes before publication. One day he telephoned me to say he was in trouble for publishing a psychological sex book. The case was dismissed and Walter Hutchinson was most grateful for my help, such as it was. I had seen detectives looking at the book in Harrods, but, when they brought the case, they had bought the copy in Charing Cross Road. I told Walter about this and said his counsel could make something of the fact that the book could have been purchased at Harrods, so why subsequently did they buy the book in the Charing Cross Road, unless it was that they were planning something of a smear tactic?

I did not study the case to see if this was an important factor in the verdict, but Walter, as I say, won and this made him a friend for life. He published one book by a well-known thriller writer but withdrew it for pulping when I said I thought it likely that an action would be brought. I still have a copy of the book—probably the only one in existence. His action was reported in the press and the police then swooped on the previous publication by the same author and a fine was imposed.

Of course not only the library and book departments in a departmental store have problems. A dead duck was received in our poultry department with the instructions, 'Please stuff this duck'; so it was carefully plucked and prepared for the table with suitable stuffing. The customer was most upset! It appeared that this was a deceased favourite, which she had had for years and wished to preserve in a glass case!

But next time the right action seemed clear. A dead canary was received in a small box with the customer's name and address. It was given to the taxidermist who stuffed it and mounted it in a glass case. Wrong again! The canary had been bought by the customer a few days before and had died almost immediately, so she had sent it back for an autopsy. She was not amused.

One can easily get lost in these large departmental stores with their complex system of tunnels and stockrooms under ground: so much so that, in one instance, a member of the staff actually 'lived' in the basement for months and had set himself up with a bed, bookcase, wardrobe and bedside lamp. Curiously enough he had been singled out for dismissal

Field-Marshal Sir Claude Auchinleck talking to the author. The life-sized picture of Rommel in the background gives the illusion that he is actually there looking on

A Golden Wedding picture of F. S. Thornton, the Oxford bookseller, and his wife, in 1952

Thomas Alfred Joy, President of the Booksellers Association of
Great Britain & Ireland, in 1957

merely because he would insist on wearing plimsolls! I assume that he wore them to enable him to creep about at night. He confessed to the staff manager that he had a system of 'clocking out', returning and missing the night watchmen. I said that, instead of being dismissed, he should have been recruited to the 'security staff' as he was an obvious expert.

Only once did I know of a customer being locked in the store overnight and in this instance she was mentally deranged. Suffering from domestic troubles and having no-where to go, the poor soul thought of the store she loved as a kind of second home. She hid herself there at closing time.

Every precaution is taken, but I am surprised that not more people are locked in. What is not generally known is that shutters and other security or fire precaution arrangements operate as soon as the store is closed and the telephones are useless as each store has its own telephone switch-board which if manned all night does not deal with internal telephones. There could be worse places in which to spend a night! You would certainly have food in great variety, books to read, even beds to lie on after, say, an alcoholic tour of the wine cellars! Undressed models, sometimes minus a limb, would be rather macabre companions, and strange gurgling in the complexity of pipes, rats and the odd pigeon or sparrow trapped in the building might disturb your slumbers.

During the war years a number of us slept in Harrods basement. We were on night duty, firewatching. The only things I found intolerable were boredom and the snoring of my companions!

As book-buyer for Harrods, I was something of a power in the book world and soon became acquainted with many famous authors, some of whom became life-long friends like Dennis Wheatley, Sir Arthur Bryant, Godfrey Winn, Catherine Gaskin and Somerset Maugham, who invited me to his villa in the South of France and Harry Price, who invited me to the haunted Borley Rectory—foolishly I never went to either. Then I met many war heroes, escapers like

Eric Williams, who wrote *The Wooden Horse*, still the best escape story of the last war, Russell Braddon, Peter Churchill, who married Odette, and many others.

From time to time I was asked for advice and one such instance had a tragic ending. Erica Beale was writing a life of King George V called *King Emperor* and asked me to read the manuscript. At our last interview in my office at Harrods, I told her my views and we argued about certain points. That night she was killed in an air-raid. Her mother asked me to complete the book but I explained that I was reluctant to alter it in any way as Erica had views which differed from my own. She then said that just a few hours before her death, Erica had mentioned this conversation with me and had decided that I was right, so I completed the work which was published by Collins in 1941. Erica had already kindly acknowledged my help in the 'Acknowledgements', but I treasure a letter of thanks I had from her mother. It is this kind of service which I, in common with other booksellers, are only too happy to give.

Life is never dull in the bookshop of departmental stores. The public can make the most extraordinary mistakes regarding titles of books, for instance, *Love in a Cold Bath* (*Climate*) by Nancy Mitford, *How Green was My Valet* (*Valley*) by Richard Llewellyn, and *The Son is My Undoing* (*Sun*) by Marguerite Steen. A mail order extract came to us once for a book called '*Undiscovered Ends*', but the clerk deciphered it as *Uncle's Covered Ends*. We received a letter from a schoolboy as follows, 'My sister has had *Fun in the Country* and now wants *More Fun in the Country*, can you supply it?' More than one customer actually received turnip tops when it was the *book* of that title by Ethel Boileau which was required, but I was fully prepared in the case of *The Wooden Horse* and told the mail order department to be careful to send books, not wooden horses. Wrong again! We received a complaint because a wooden horse *was* wanted as a birthday gift for a boy of eight, and in the customer's opinion the book was 'hardly suitable reading for one of his age'. There has since been published a 'cadet' edition for the younger reader.

All kinds of things are used as book-markers. We found pocket combs, ten shilling and one pound notes and, once, no less than five one pound notes. On one occasion a sheet of comic verses turned up, one of which I thought particularly good. It went:

> It nearly broke her father's heart
> When Lady Madge became a tart.
> But blood is blood and race is race
> And so to save the Ducal face
> He bought her the most expensive beat
> From Lower to Upper Berkeley Street.

Sometimes the good humour of customers can be tried to excess. One store was asked to supply a large veal-and-ham-pie for a party. Later, a rather boozy voice informed us over the telephone that, on being cut, the pie was found to be full of sawdust! It appeared that in some extraordinary way a pie made for display purposes had been sent. All the machinery to correct the error was put into motion. The cold storage was opened and a fresh pie sent off by special messenger in a taxi. Sighs of relief all round. Then the telephone rang again—another sawdust pie!

Sale time was a new experience for me and I was amazed at my first encounter with 'sale fever'. Let me say that sales in the best departmental stores are absolutely genuine and there are great bargains to be had. First, the stock generally is reduced in price and goods which have been in stock for a year or more—the period is shorter in fashion departments —are drastically reduced, often to a fraction of the actual cost. There are also buy-ins, that is to say, bargains that buyers are looking out for throughout the year to buy for the sale.

Manufacturers have oddments and models such as radio and TV sets superseded by later patterns, and they constitute real bargains when they are offered for sale. Buyers in stores are instructed to maintain the standard of merchandise when buying for the sale, so buy-ins are not rubbish but a way of disposing of manufacturers' overstock at a time when the stores are also diposing of their overstocks. Some articles, such as cut-glass, *are* actually manufactured for sales, but here again the merchandise is offered at bargain prices. I know this to be so because in due course I became merchandise manager and had an inside knowledge of what went on in each department.

'Seconds' are often offered in sales and it is clearly indicated that they are sub-standard but, remember, British standards are high and a small indentation or scratch on a shoe is sufficient to make it a 'second'. Obviously a few scratches would be inevitable in wearing, so these are bargains and the same holds good for a wide range of merchandise. The store rule was that if a reduced price was indicated it must be genuine. For instance, '30/-, sale price 10/-' would not be permissible if the goods had been manufactured for the sale and had not been genuinely offered at a higher price originally. Instead the sale ticket would read, 'Sale Bargain 10/-', no original price being indicated.

Seeing the effect in the stores, I wrote an article showing how these techniques could be used to advantage by the book trade. I mooted a National Sale Week for bookshops. Little notice was taken of the article, but it was so firmly in my mind that I used every opportunity to promote the idea of the National Sale Week. After twenty years I persuaded the booksellers at an annual conference of the Booksellers Association to try it out as an experiment and so the National Book Sale came into being. It is now an annual event, and the public respond eagerly to the book bargains made available, including some publishers' overstocks as well as booksellers' superfluous stocks. Over a quarter of a million books are sold annually at half-price or less during the National Book Sale and all this started because I was so impressed by the tremendous success of the sale periods at Harrods.

I have the pleasure, therefore, of being acclaimed the

'father' of the National Book Sale and, of course, I am proud of the title. It affords individuals and librarians the opportunity of obtaining books at bargain prices, but I suppose my greatest achievement in inaugurating book sales was the purchase for Harrods of the stock of Mudie's library. This old-established firm went out of business in 1937 and I bought up the whole stock and offered something between a half and three-quarters of a million books to the public and to Public and County Librarians for a fraction of their original cost. I gave tens of thousands of books to hospitals with the 'compliments' of Harrods, as well as making a very handsome profit for the firm and gaining a large and valuable mailing list.

But what a tragedy—that a bookselling and library business of such importance, with worldwide contacts, should be forced to close! Hundreds of people were thrown out of work and I engaged almost one hundred ex-Mudie staff to help in the sorting, cataloguing and selling of Mudie's stock. Some of this staff are still working in Harrods library, including the manager.

I stuck my neck out in buying this huge stock, with all the attendant difficulties of moving it and organising the sale, but I was supported in every way by a great chief, Cadness Page, the head librarian, who as buyer sanctioned the purchase and who would doubtless have 'carried the can' if things had not worked out. It was a triumph of optimism. I knew I had a bargain as far as the value of the stock was concerned, but the organisation and shelving of so large a quantity of books caused me a sleepless night or two. At one time it worked out that the extra shelving space available to me would take around 30,000 volumes but I had bought over *half a million*. By replanning and by getting some basement space it worked out in the end. But what a fright! Looking back I am amazed at my own temerity. Youth has something in its very make-up which is an ingredient of success. Life has taught me that experience is of extreme value but the incaution of youth is also of value.

That is why I, and many others, conclude that a good board of Directors, for instance, should be composed of older experienced people and a few young trouble-shooters who must be tolerated and liked, in spite of their own intolerance of their elders and of their belligerency. Youth does not 'wrap it up', often because it does not know how. Diplomacy is not an attribute of youth. In these days when British management is often criticised, I look back with some wonder and gratitude for the tolerance and vision of the management with whom I dealt, and I have come to regard British top management as the finest in the world. Middle management, due doubtless to the wastage of the war years tends all too often to be weak.

I had been at Harrods library for only a brief time before war was declared. Harrods library had well over 15,000 members who paid a subscription to receive the latest books on publication. Obviously the library would become jammed unless the unwanted books were sold at roughly the same rate as books were purchased and my job was to sell this surplus stock. It is bought largely by public and county librarians, so ratepayers benefit, as libraries buy this stock at a fraction of the published price.

To meet the demands of subscribers, perhaps over one thousand copies of a title or even more are bought in advance of publication and within a few weeks the demand has largely been met. All the copies would be circulating for a week or two but the demand gradually lessens and surplus copies accumulate ready to be sold six months after publication at a reduced price.

To help accomplish this we had four representatives calling on libraries all over England, Scotland and Ireland to take orders.

After I had been a year at Harrods, the Hon. Andrew Shirley left, as he had been appointed head librarian of the Times Library, and I was appointed deputy librarian in his place. The library was a gay place with around sixty young lady assistants and a total staff of around one hundred. I was in my element!

How can you control so large a staff? is a question often asked. I have already commented on management, giving conclusions based on my personal experience and observation. In my Army & Navy Stores days I had a staff of well over one thousand, and my short answer to the question is that one manages oneself. Self-discipline is all important. One must not lose one's temper, must endeavour to be patient, scrupulously just and not have favourites. Even so, it is difficult, as one has human weaknesses and in a time of ill-health—even a headache—one's judgment is impaired. One must expect one's motives to be misunderstood, as for instance when dealing with personal problems, where the confidence of the individual cannot be betrayed and one is therefore handicapped by not being in a position to explain.

For example, one may know from the firm's doctor that an assistant is seriously ill, which accounts, say, for her lethargy and unpunctuality; but even the patient may not be aware of the seriousness of her illness so, as nothing can be divulged, she is apparently 'getting away with it'.

Management is indeed an art and only in part can it be taught. At top level management is, in my experience, overall sound and humane, but improvement is necessary in much middle management. All too often 'down the line' one finds the immature, small-minded approach. A second or third in command is much more likely to stand on his dignity, throw his weight about, 'gun' for anyone who opposes him in any way, and, feeling frustrated, be disloyal to his immediate superiors. One must therefore not only discipline oneself but control and lead the under-managers. It is a good rule never to be sarcastic or over-familiar. 'Familiarity breeds contempt', but I was surprised when a young lady pointed out that although this was true, it was equally true that without it one could not breed at all!

I continued to learn lessons in management at Harrods, particularly during the war years when my chief, Cadness

Page, was serving in the forces, where he was ultimately promoted from the ranks as a Territorial volunteer to Major. It was in his absence that I took control as Manager of the library and book department throughout the war. During these years we sent thousands of book parcels to prisoners of war and books to libraries such as the Royal Naval War Libraries, the Red Cross, and so on.

In the war years, as manager, I had the honour of attending from time to time H.M. The Queen who brought with her Princess Elizabeth and Princess Margaret.

Both during and after working hours most of us were Air Raid Wardens and both worked and slept on the premises. There were, of course, plenty of 'incidents' and my office was destroyed by a flying bomb, but no one was hurt. The extraordinary thing was that the blast blew out the windows and triangular pieces of glass pierced right through some of the books. For some time I had them on view as 'war souvenirs'.

We were so bored sometimes that we took chances and walked out into the blitz and blacked-out streets or went to the cinema in off-duty hours. So much has been written of the courage of Londoners in the blitz that I will not dwell on it other than to say that I, like all who lived through it, ended the war not only with enhanced national pride but with wonder at the incredible courage and spirit of the average Londoner.

Almost every day we learned that some member of the staff had been killed or injured or their homes had been destroyed. One member of the staff fell, while on firewatching duty, from the top of Harrods and we found his body in the street. The roof and ledges on top of the building were something of a maze and in certain places it was possible to climb a wall and drop down to take a short cut. I imagine the poor fellow made a mistake and dropped where there was no ledge.

I was lucky and often missed death by a narrow margin. When Harrods garage was destroyed, my little Austin was the only car to come out absolutely untouched; all the expensive, beautiful cars were burned out. I was in the habit of parking outside a Knightsbridge pub where I spent some hours playing darts when not on duty. One night a bomb dropped almost on my parking spot; it destroyed the pub and killed those who were in it, but I was not there. I was lucky.

Somehow we managed to keep the library service running and the store generally carried on, whatever the difficulties. Food and goods were scarce, books were 'rationed' by the publishers but fortunately we had a very large stock to start with, which helped. I was summoned to advise the War Office, where I was interviewed by Ian Hay, on books to be supplied to the troops, and also had other interviews to advise regarding books to be sent for the other services. This in part was the beginning of the library services, now fully established, to meet the needs of serving personnel. Comforts for the troops, particularly in the form of books, were not deemed necessary by all in command and one had therefore no little opposition when advising that libraries could and should be provided.

Another interesting task I was asked to perform was to look out the most valuable books in the library of the Junior Carlton Club in order that they could be removed to a place of safety. This came about, I believe, because the Carlton Club opposite had received a direct hit and most of the library was destroyed and to avoid a similar happening to the Junior Carlton Club library, it was thought advisable to take this course. In fact, fighter aircraft were attacking enemy planes as I proceeded to examine and select the books which had particular interest or value.

Staff would willingly work overtime to prepare parcels of books for prisoners of war. Tens of thousands of books were despatched and prisoners could study or read for pleasure as a result. My staff were constantly changing as they volunteered or were called to serve, so constant training of new staff was necessary to maintain an efficient service. In the library alone, I recorded 1,500 changes and by the end of the war, the average age of assistants must have been between fifty and sixty.

I regard the maintenance of Harrods library service during the war as my greatest achievement, though no one but myself knows all that it entailed. By the end of hostilities I was extremely tired and ill and badly needed to rest after the stress and strain of those years.

I decided to leave Harrods, when my chief was released from the service. Fortunately the book department manager of the Army & Navy Stores had reached retiring age, so I applied for the position and was accepted and appointed manager and buyer of the book department, beginning at the end of October 1945.

It was agreed furthermore that I should start a circulating library there in addition to my duties as book department manager and this appealed to me enormously. To start a subscription library from scratch in one of London's leading stores was a challenge and just what I needed to inspire me to renewed efforts. It was hard to leave Harrods, which had done so much for me and where I had so many friends, but the time had come, I felt, to make the break.

A new job is a challenge, it keeps you young, but change is rarely comfortable. One is, as it were, again on trial and a lot of one's heart is still with friends and colleagues in the old firm. Each time I have changed positions it has proved to be for the best, as far as I can judge, but the process was usually painful. Many people stay in the same job or in the same firm all their lives and who is to say that they are wrong? It is a matter of temperament, and I suppose ambition is linked with it. To some people there comes a desire for 'fresh woods and pastures new'.

The changes I made in my career were usually made at roughly ten year intervals, by which time I felt I had made the contribution I could make and could probably do more elsewhere. The all important thing is to know one's capabilities and one's limitations, no easy thing to assess, and then courageously to make the change when what seems to be the right opening appears. It is said, 'Opportunity knocks only once!' In my experience it rarely knocks at all, it is a shadowy figure slinking past almost without visible shape and form. One must recognise it nevertheless, and grab it or it will slip by, probably for good.

X

When recounting amusing and interesting book trade experiences, people say, 'You must write a book about it.' But many such experiences cannot be recounted, as living personalities are involved and although we in the trade understand one another and can tell stories about our friends and their idiosyncrasies we are, as it were, a family and family talk does no harm as long as it is *kept in the family*.

Booksellers and publishers are truly very much 'a family' —much more so than people in most other trades. We meet at countless publishers' parties and once a year at the Conference, where the social life is, if anything, more important than the business sessions. Over the years one gets to know every bookseller of importance throughout Great Britain and Ireland and their wives. By 'importance' one does not necessarily mean those who own or control large businesses, but those who are 'important' because they contribute to Conference discussions, or write letters and articles in the trade press and serve on various committees of the Booksellers Association. In short it is personality plus character which brings a bookseller or publisher into 'the family'. To some extent this 'family' is international, and we are received with warmth and hospitality all over the world by fellow bookmen.

It is pleasing to find on one's travels not only in Europe but as far afield as the United States, Bermuda, Africa, the Bahamas, Scandinavia and even in more remote parts, that almost every bookseller knows of one's activities mainly through photographs and reports in the trade press, in *The Bookseller* or *Smith's Trade News* or, less frequently, in the national press. Booksellers and publishers read avidly all the trade papers, all the trade gossip columns, reviews and book advertisements, so we keep in touch not only with the new books but with one another.

Over many years it has been customary for all prominent London booksellers to be photographed for publicity purposes with provincial and other booksellers and authors in the news. The purpose of these photographs, most of which are taken at publishers' parties and autographing sessions— autographing sessions are part of a bookseller's life—is simply publicity for a new book not for the individuals photographed. Authors and publishers feel, rightly or wrongly, that a picture of an author with leading trade personalities has publicity value. I was once photographed talking to Field-Marshal Sir Claude Auchinleck against a background of Arab tents and a picture of General Erwin Rommel. The effect was so realistic that when the photograph appeared in *Illustrated* it looked as if I was in serious conference over military matters at top level! This picture was good fun and appreciated in the trade as such, but it may well have enlarged my cosmopolitan reputation as some time after the publication of the picture I received a request from someone in Nigeria offering me a large quantity of ground nuts and some snake or monkey skins—I forget which—in return for books. One such person wrote to one of my old bosses offering one of his wives in exchange for books. My boss was not amused but his staff were, and the jokes about possibilities were varied and 'blue'. It pays to advertise!

Any bookseller, whatever his colour or creed, is made welcome by his fellows to a degree of friendly warmth which, as I have said, does not exist in other trades. As a director of the Army & Navy Stores, I have travelled on business to research into methods of marketing in departmental stores at home and abroad, and in the store world at top level there is no lack of co-operation; you are welcome to ask any questions and see all that interests you.

It is true that the store chiefs also meet on various committees, work together and meet socially, so the book trade is, in this respect, not unique; but bookselling is a smaller 'world' and therefore more intimate, so much so that quite junior assistants will be able to meet many of the leading trade figures and quickly become known themselves as trade personalities. Bookselling, I often say, is a disease— once it is in the blood you can never lose it. People who leave the trade, for whatever reason—perhaps, if they are young women, to get married—will try to return to it sooner or later and they always say how much they have missed their contacts in the book world.

Booksellers in and around the London area have advantages over those in scattered areas and there is surely no trade with so many publicity parties. These parties are very useful as well as being enjoyable functions as they often kindle an enthusiasm for the writer and his subject. They introduce the author and his new book and one usually comes away from a party better informed than one would otherwise be and this enables one to get the 'feel' of the market.

Booksellers, particularly London booksellers, are from time to time invited to see a preview of a new film based on a book and they may meet the stars taking part in it. This has considerable trade value, so much so that not only owners and managers of bookshops are invited but assistants too, since after all they are the ones who sell the book and contact the film-going public. Books are obviously particularly interesting to buy and sell and the constant stream of new titles adds zest to the life of everyone in the trade.

It is hard work for bookshop assistants, as well as the managers, to keep abreast and they must read a lot to keep themselves informed about books. They must know not only the current year's publications but those of past years, and have advance information regarding books not yet issued. In Britain everyone is helped by having the best possible reference books. The weekly publication *The Bookseller* lists under alphabetical order both title and author of all the books published in Great Britain during that week, and then in a similar way, all the books published during the month. All this is put together to appear quarterly until, finally, all the books published during the year are available in two alphabetical arrangements, one under authors and one under titles. This information is supplemented by issues of lists of forthcoming books, also of paperbacks in print, and most valuable of all, 'The Bible' of the book trade, a yearly publication entitled *British Books in Print*. This title clearly explains the contents.

It is most important to have reference books 'centralised' in the bookshop. There are some assistants whose excellent memories can carry a store of data, past, present and future, but all must in some measure rely on reference books. Book-knowledge is first built up by actually handling and living with books, but linked with this is the reading of trade journals etc.

There are many other important 'tools of the trade' which make it possible for booksellers to answer almost any question about books; and this service, by the way, is one which the public expects absolutely free of charge, although both the reference books and the time spent in research are costly. Similarly a bookseller is expected to order any book not in stock, though when a book is specially ordered little or no profit is made, particularly if research has to be made to trace the publisher from whom the book must be ordered. Today some booksellers find it necessary to make a charge for special orders.

Authors naturally like to see their books on display in the bookshops but it simply is not possible for a bookseller to have a copy of everything in stock, since some 300,000 British books are in print. But to an author *his* book is all important. However, a bookseller's reputation depends on three things; the satisfaction of his buying public and, to some extent, of authors and of publishers.

The concern of authors is very understandable and a few lesser authors do a bit of private snooping, sometimes being positively belligerent in their complaints not only to the bookseller but to their publishers that their books are not in stock or on display. It is really unfair to demand of some poor bookshop manager or assistant, 'Why is my book not on show?' A little thought on the author's part would make him or her realise that this omission works in two ways. After all, if the author's book is all too visible it may well be because it is not selling. On the other hand, if it is missing, then such copies as were in stock could have been sold and more will be coming in.

Bookshop assistants need to be enthusiastic and gifted salesmen, not simply assistants who can find a book on the shelves and wrap it up when told. An assistant who replies airily, 'It's out of print, I'm afraid,' and has no reliable basis for this statement is a menace in any shop.

There are courses of training up to management level for those employed in bookselling and almost all the assistants I first met when I came to London in 1935 became managers as the years passed. It is a trade with prospects, even if progress tends to be slow.

But bookselling is by no means the quiet, clean, light job it appears to be to those outside the trade. Parcels of books from the publishers are heavy, books readily gather dust and the knowledge of books required makes it an exacting business. In all it can be exasperating at times, but the fun lies in the perpetual challenge the trade offers. There is no clear road to the top. So much depends on the personality of the individual and a good deal on the perception and imagination of those above you.

A good manager needs to have a personal contact with his staff; reliance on hearsay is not the same thing. It is important to be 'on the floor', particularly at busy times, and to watch points. This way, promising staff can be spotted, and they can then be given a freer hand, with an opportunity to express their creative abilities in the building up of stock, preparation of displays etc. The manager must spot talent, to prevent the more intelligent and promising assistant being channelled into mainly routine jobs.

Potential booksellers need patience and determination as well as a good education, a wide and insatiable love of literature (quick readers with quick minds and retentive memories are most useful in the book trade), open-minded curiosity about everything and a gift for spotting not only promising staff but best-sellers! Also for spotting unusual 'winners'—publications that every Tom, Dick and Harry will not want, but that are likely 'winners' in their own specialised field, having appeal to a special or to the more discerning public.

The good book-salesman needs to apply common-sense pyschology. The mind of each customer can be tactfully explored and his or her tastes assessed. Some customers like to be left to browse, but watch *what* they buy and you can often extend their purchases or offer them something that pleases them the next time they come, and there *will* be a next time if you are clever. One must be helpful, but not pushing. One must sell a book with the conviction that the customer will truly like it and, above all, one must be kind to the timid shopper and never be priggish about any publication.

Booksellers are not arbiters of taste, but they must preserve their own standards and cultivate personal enthusiasm. This will always come through to the customer. In this way you encourage 'regulars', who always come to you for guidance.

The fitting of the right book to the right need is a most satisfying experience and it is this that makes bookselling a vocation, not just a job.

What could be more rewarding than to introduce to a child a book he will remember all his life or to an adult a book which will give pleasure, to a sportsman, a book on his favourite sport that he did not know existed, or to introduce a new book on religion which gives a new interpretation or one which strengthens faith?

Or again to recommend maps and guides to help holiday makers to select wisely and to make the best of their holidays? One could go on endlessly listing reasons why bookselling performs a function to the community as important and in some ways more important than that of the public libraries. Those people who go regularly into bookshops, browse around and buy are fortunate indeed. The opportunity is there for all, but some people need guidance to appreciate that a richer, fuller life is impossible without books.

People often say that books are dear but in fact British books are very cheap—cheap, that is, if compared with other forms of recreation and entertainment. A seat at a theatre or West End cinema costs as much as a beautiful hardback book, but the book can give *lasting* pleasure. A small box of chocolates costs as much or more than a good paperback. A snack meal costs as much as many a good book. Improvements in the printing and making of books have kept prices down and relatively speaking books are cheaper today than pre-war.

Going back a hundred years or so a book could cost as much as a farm labourer's weekly wage. A farm labourer could buy a library of books for his weekly wage today, which I hope proves my point that books are cheap.

Bookselling is no quick way to making a fortune; indeed many booksellers find it difficult even to make a living. There are many reasons why this is so; but the main one is that of stock difficulty. A butcher sells his meat once a week or more. A grocer and provision merchant turns his stock over at a reasonable rate and although every form of retailing has its own peculiar difficulties few, if any, have the same problem in the same measure as a bookseller, who has somehow to select stock from the 35,000 odd new titles each year and select stock that will sell. However skilled he may be, however good his flair, he will make mistakes and books which do not sell are all too often a dead loss, reducing his profits accordingly. Some titles go on selling for years but the demand for others disappears almost overnight. A TV programme will suddenly stimulate sales of a title and sometimes it is a nine days' wonder. TV and radio have had a great influence on book sales and the trade has much to thank them for. The interest aroused in archaeology by the Mortimer Wheeler programmes, the Lord (Kenneth) Clark programmes and many others come to mind, as does, of course, 'Going for a Song' with Arthur Negus, which stimulated interest in antiques generally. All these have written their own best-sellers too, to the benefit of booksellers and public alike.

The enormously successful TV presentation of Galsworthy's *The Forsyte Saga* revived this work as a best-seller years after its original publication. The dramatisations of the Thomas Hardy, George Eliot and Henry James novels presented on the television screen led to an immediate demand for the books themselves and so the influence of TV has helped booksellers, quite contrary to what the 'dismal Jimmies' prophesied. In TV they saw the end of book-reading, whereas on the contrary it has stimulated it. This dismal outlook which is all too common, persists over the years in spite of so much evidence to the contrary. Radio did not, as was prophesied, kill the gramophone record, quite the reverse. The long-playing record did not ruin the record manufacturers as was predicted; again quite the reverse. But to be a pessimist seems to be more popular than to be a 'pop-eyed optimist'. 'All is for the best in the best of all possible worlds' and I go along with this wisdom of Voltaire's *Candide*. *Candide* together with Boccaccio's *Decameron*, Defoe's *Moll Flanders*, and *The Golden Ass of Lucius Apuleius*, are books I read and read again. I needed them first as 'textbooks' because of their important place in the development of the novel, but I grew to love them. I still read and love the Sherlock Holmes stories and Rider Haggard; they read as well today as in my youth. Omar Khayyam influenced me in my teens but I have grown away from him. These books in particular, and of course many others, have, I believe, helped to give me a cheerful philosophy of life for which I am grateful.

Booksellers have been alarmed by so many changes over

the last fifty years but unnecessarily so. Book Clubs, it was thought, would interfere with the selling of books at full price. The Book Society would, it was feared, tend to keep book buyers out of the bookshops, where once they could be tempted to extend their purchases. Book Tokens, invented by a publisher, Harold Raymond, were initially opposed by many as it was thought they would sell more readily than books, particularly in the Christmas season, and although they would ultimately be exchanged for books, these might be textbooks on which there is a smaller margin of profit than those usually selected to be given as Christmas presents. Above all, it was feared paperbacks would become more popular than the more costly hardbacks. All these fears were groundless. Paperbacks increased reading as a habit and hardback sales are now better than ever. Book Tokens, too, have increased the sale of books by putting un-bookish buyers on a safe wicket when they buy for their bookish friends and diverting them from other articles which they might regard as safer buys.

Book Clubs encourage reading and home libraries since, to sum up, 'One good book leads to another'—in whatever form you buy it.

When I first advocated the National Book Sale, I was accused of cheapening the trade. Sales, it was said, were un-dignified in good class bookshops. It was feared that people would wait for the Sale and not buy in the weeks before. They would become satiated with sale purchases and not buy in the weeks following. These arguments cannot all be dismissed as nonsense but in practice the adverse effects are small in comparison with the advantages. A sale's first object is to bring people into the shop who might otherwise not have entered and, once they are there, to persuade them to see not only the bargains but the tempting range of books on the shelves, which they may buy subsequently, if not at the time. Secondly, everyone likes a bargain, and goodwill is built up by having really genuine ones. Finally one clears unwanted stock simply by having thousands of extra customers in the shop with diverse interests, who pick up books on their pet subjects and buy them because they are going cheap. Many books sold in the sales at bargain prices have since become scarce and would fetch very much more today than the price paid for them. The public always arrives hopefully at a sale and the book trade need be no exception to retailing generally, where annual or twice yearly sales benefit both customer and shopkeeper.

Publishers, like booksellers, also have overstocks. A publisher has to guess at the number of copies of a book he should print or re-print at a time. 'Guess' is hardly the word, as his printing figure is based on his experience, nevertheless each book is different and the past sales of an author are not an infallible yardstick, since his new book, which may be quite different in style from his previous ones, may sell in greater or lesser quantities.

First books by new authors are obviously more difficult to assess than a new book by a well-known author, particularly if the author sticks to the mixture as before.

The larger the printing order, the cheaper the cost of each copy, so a publisher is tempted to place the largest possible order and from time to time he is over optimistic and his warehouse fills up with hundreds or thousands of copies of books which will sell slowly, if at all. Naturally he would like to turn this stock into cash to enable him to publish still more books. There is the space problem too.

The National Book Sale is arranged to take these publishers' overstocks into the bookshop and offer them in the sale generally at half the published price or less. These books are in new condition and liven up the slightly shop-soiled books which the bookseller can offer from his own stock.

The National Book Sale, as held in Britain, is unique, no country in the world having an exact parallel. The best bargains are, of course, available during the first day or two of the sale, but on the last two days anything left is usually offered at 'give-away' prices. So it is worth having a last fling on these days for unrepeatable bargains.

Bookshops are as important to the cultural life of a town as a public library, but ratepayers and librarians are not as conscious of this as booksellers would like them to be. It is difficult and sometimes impossible to run a bookshop at a profit unless books for the local library are bought, at least in part, from the local bookseller. Even so the bookseller must give a 10% discount to public libraries and this severely reduces his profits.

Public librarians can and frequently do place the larger part of their orders with library suppliers. There are a variety of reasons for this, but in some countries this would not be permitted as the politicians legislate to ensure the prosperity of bookshops, appreciating their national importance. A librarian would argue that the library supplier has larger stocks than his local bookshop and this may be true, but it is equally true that the local bookseller could and would have a larger stock if he had more of the library business. Again the librarian likes the supplier of the library books to do what should be work for his own library staff. Librarians commonly expect the bookseller to insert library labels and pockets and protective jackets to be placed round the original jacket. The labour involved often presents a real difficulty to the small bookseller, who undertakes the work in order to compete with larger firms of library suppliers, although it is likely to prove uneconomic.

A librarian would argue that he must buy in the best market and safeguard the ratepayers' money; but he would serve the community better by being more community-minded and by doing all in his power to support the local bookseller. The whole public library system seems to me to be in considerable need of overhauling; individual librarians apparently buy what they consider to be the most popular books in order to keep up the number of issues, rather than buying books truly needed locally to meet the needs of the more serious readers. Too many trashy novels are purchased and money is wasted on ephemeral literature.

Children's libraries are tremendously important and

nothing should stand in the way of their development; here one gives credit where it is due because public libraries have done a splendid job. A local library should, I feel, first gear itself to meet the needs of the locality; for instance, if the area contains, say, a steel works or teaching hospital, then the needs of the students and workers should be met. The local library should be strong on books of the home county and on books connected with the history, flora and fauna of the locality. Of course, most good librarians have, over the years, been conscious of these requirements, and have met them to some extent, but after the last war (books were scarce in the war years and as a consequence people flocked to public libraries), some librarians, it seemed to me, followed Parkinson's Law. How could they best meet and improve demand, as a falling off would make their jobs appear less important? So they bought, at the ratepayers' expense, more and more books to amuse the masses. Therefore today many people get all their recreational reading and, in some places, gramophone records too, from the local library. Of course, gramophone record libraries offer a serious cultural service, together with the lending of musical scores, but how far should all this go without charging some fee to those using the service? The books and records are costly but in addition there is the cost of the organization and the premises. It seems unjust that those ratepayers who do not use the facilities are subsidising people who often could, and would be, willing to *pay* for them.

The commercial libraries are dying, Boots's great lending library is gone, so too has Smith's and the Times, as well as most of the old twopenny libraries. The public libraries killed them, together with the advent of paperbacks which I think must also have been a contributory factor.

In the circumstances it is remarkable that bookshops can succeed at all when the books they stock can be borrowed free. How many television sets, radios or gas stoves would be sold if they were obtainable free from the local authority?

From all this, the conclusion might be drawn that I am

against public libraries whereas, like all booksellers, I am all for them, but I would like to see Britain become more a book-buying rather than a book-borrowing country and to educate more people to want to possess books. Libraries both help and hinder bookselling. I am sure they help by creating and fostering the reading habit but their function should, I believe, not include the supplying of the latest relatively unimportant books. Thrillers, westerns, romances and the like should be available, but to a restricted degree, and the same applies to a lot of non-fiction. It is a bookseller talking, but many people with no financial interest in the trade or books agree with me and deplore the *free* supply of books of little merit.

Bookselling is rather more profitable than it was just before the turn of the century, when many leading bookshops had to close their doors as discount on books had reached un-economic proportions. This was before the Net Book Agreement. This agreement effectively retains net prices or, in other words, it ensures that books are sold only at the full price to the public. Educational books which are mainly sold to schools are sold at a discount at practically no profit to the bookseller and even net books are sold to public and certain other libraries at a ten per cent discount. But the man in the street pays the full price for a new book wherever he shops and paradoxically he gets best value in this way. At a first glance if a person buying a book could get something off the price he would get a cheaper book, but that is not how it would work. All the evidence on this issue was heard in the Restrictive Practices Court in October 1962, where, in a reserved judgment, it was declared, 'The restrictions in the Net Book Agreement were not contrary to the public interest.' The Court found that the abrogation of the Agreement would result in fewer and less well-equipped stock-holding bookshops, *more expensive books* and fewer published titles.

It is certain that book prices would rise dramatically if discounts were given. This is because book prices are largely governed by the number of copies which are printed and this printing number is, in its turn, governed by the advance orders. Booksellers would order the smallest possible number of each title if they thought competitors would be selling at a discount, consequently publishers' printing orders would be lower and up would go the price. It is not generally appreciated how disastrous this would be, not only to the book trade but to the country as a whole. Books are, in themselves, one of our great exports and bring in additional cash for film rights, radio and television rights, translation rights and serialisation fees. But most important, they introduce to the whole world the British way of life, our history, tradition and countryside and this brings the tourists. By reading our history books and historical novels, and seeing plays set in Britain, people want to visit the places depicted. The Brontë country, Stratford-upon-Avon, Scotland, Wales, even Baker Street with its Sherlock Holmes association, are all places tourists come to see. How long would this last and in what reduced measure, were British books not available abroad? That they *are* available is because, in spite of keen American competition, they are relatively cheap. If prices jumped up the market would be lost to our competitors and, in time Britain could become if not a forgotten country, one not as popular, one not so important in the minds of the tourists. Many people will think I exaggerate but I believe all this could come about were it not for the protection afforded by the Net Book Agreement.

True or false, it is better to be on the safe side than to risk so much—for what?

Once let the economic wizards get at the book trade and like the railways, coal-mines, public transport, all of which made profits under private enterprise, the industry would soon be ruined. I am, alas, old enough to recall the arguments that it was not fair that the coal in the ground should be dug up to make profits for the mine owners. 'The coal belonged to the people so the profits should go to the country to reduce taxation.' Where are the profits now? The taxpayer has to put his hand into his pocket to subsidise the mines and the railways and the users pay more and more but still no profit is made. Politics? Maybe, but the lesson is a grim one.

Young people today in this more affluent society are able and eager to buy books. They do so more and more and thus increase their knowledge and pleasure. What a great stride forward this is and in it lies the hope for the future with greater happiness, richer and fuller lives. We also need to take education, which is impossible without books, to the backward peoples of the world if we are to bring understanding and peace.

Bookselling is, as I have said, more than a trade; it is a vocation and a noble one. Lucky are the people engaged in it and lucky indeed was I when, so very early in life, my steps were guided in this direction, through reading at home and also through the kindness of my school friend, Bobby Butler (son of the Registrar in Worcester Street, Oxford), who had the best library of children's books of any of my friends, including bound volumes of the *Strand Magazine* with the Sherlock Holmes stories. I almost lived there at his home, reading, having gorgeous teas and a book or two to take home to read. Later I joined the Bivouac Club, which had the most comprehensive library in Oxford of books for boys, provided free by the kindness of Dr Henderson, the Roman historian, and a medical doctor, Dr Ormerod. The local public library did not attract me so much, as the books were all re-bound uniformly in dull covers, which gave no guidance as to the contents, and lost them their individuality. So I wanted to be with books. I do not think I cared much in those early days if it was likely to be a remunerative career, but it was one I liked. 'What a pity!' said a well-known citizen of Oxford, who was present at the time I signed my indenture in a solicitor's office. He did not know that I overheard his remark, but I did, and it worried me for years afterwards. It did not help, but it was a challenge to prove him wrong. He, of course, knew nothing of bookselling and probably thought it was a pity that I did not continue with my schooling and go on to the university.

There are many with university degrees in both publishing and bookselling and rightly so, but there are also many in top positions who are largely self-educated; so although it is a great asset to have a degree it does not necessarily mean greater success. Nevertheless if I could live it all again, I would certainly like first to have the three years or so at an English university and a further year at the Sorbonne, and a still further year or so at an American university. There is so much one would like to know and as I grow older I am more and more conscious of my ignorance and limitations. How far I would have been better equipped for bookselling, I do not know. Some of my friends who worked with me at Bodley took their degrees and became librarians in Oxford; two had been to Bedford House School and I meet them at the annual Old Boys Dinner. Comparisons are odious. I am sure they enjoyed their lives as I have mine, and they have been no less successful but I ponder on why it is that with similar beginnings and almost identical opportunities we all go varying ways.

Just recently, as I walked one weekend along the towpath at Medley in Oxford, I began talking to a fisherman about fishing when I was a boy. It transpired that he began at the same school as I (St Frideswides) under the same headmaster, a Mr Wigg, but he said he was quite illiterate and it had been a great handicap in his job on the railway, which he had managed to retain only by learning answers off by heart. He was a nice chap and seemed happy enough. I noticed his fishing reel, which was a very expensive one, and one which I had concluded some weeks earlier I could not afford. 'Education is a wonderful thing' as the maid replied when her mistress reprovingly said that she could write her name on the dusty shelves. But obviously a measure of prosperity and happiness does not necessarily rely on it.

XI

Departmental stores have a fascination of their own and this story of my life would not be complete unless I included a 'peep behind the scenes' of store life as I experienced it over the last thirty years or so.

A huge store is, in many ways, like a theatre. The displays are glamorous and lighting effects are designed to make the goods as attractive as possible, but behind the scenes there is less glamour, and in the older stores that is the understatement of all understatements. There are old stock-rooms, and long, dirty, ill-lighted passages which are very off-putting to new staff. It is necessary in large stores with hundreds, or even thousands, of employees for the general staff to have a staff entrance, otherwise they could walk in and out with the customers and take away goods for which they had not paid. The staff entrance serves many other purposes, including the recording of attendance and time-keeping, as well as 'security' of the company's goods.

Most stores, not only in England but all over the world, have some system intended to minimize theft by members of the staff and frequently staff have to agree to be searched; this is included in the Staff Rule Book and terms of engagement. Generally staff understand the necessity for this rule and if it is sensibly applied with no possibility of planting or victimisation, it works well and, although irksome, protects the staff. But some people find this rule so objectionable that they will not work in a departmental store.

Newcomers to stores are given a staff training course in a special department for the purpose. This is not, as many think, to teach them their job, as they will learn this in the department in which they will work, if they do not already know it, but rather to indoctrinate them by a series of lectures on the history of the firm, its trading policy and tradition. It also teaches them 'the system', that is, how to use the till, how to make out a bill or a credit note, how to deal with returned goods, and how to handle a complaining customer. Telephone courtesy and how to sell and display goods are usually covered, but the real advantage of these classes is to help one to feel at home and to make friends.

At Harrods I went through staff training as many of us did, however important our individual appointments might be. This was a splendid and most useful beginning, particularly to someone, like myself, who had never worked in a store before. Miss Jean McKay then head of the staff training department was one of the most efficient businesswomen I have ever met, and during my management years became a most friendly and helpful colleague.

Of course, one must not, as a manager, allow oneself to be ruled or overruled by the stores staff office. The staff managers have their own function, which is to deal with a variety of staff matters and to interview applicants and sift them before passing them through to the head of the department where there is a vacancy; but the selection of staff and its control is the function of the manager of the department. Here I should explain that the terms 'manager' and 'buyer' are frequently synonymous and mean the head of a department. These terms are misused and lead to much confusion both in and outside the store world. I have met people who say they were buyers at Harrods because they did in fact buy, but that does not necessarily mean that they held the rank of head buyer manager.

In my day the manager buyer was boss, almost in the same way as he would be if he owned and managed his own business. He decided on the goods to be stocked and the number of staff required to sell it and there was *no* interference from the top. In fact one was expected to have 'the feel' of the store in which one worked and to buy the quality of goods for which that particular store had a reputation.

Harrods, Selfridge's, Barkers, Debenham & Freebody, Dickins & Jones, Harvey Nichols, all these famous departmental stores have their own tradition and trade in quality goods, but they are all different. The soft furnishings of Liberty's are famous; the wine cellars of the Army & Navy Stores are world renowned; Harrods's Food Halls and many of its other departments are unrivalled. So it goes on, and a buyer taking charge of any department in any one of these stores must not only be an expert in his or her own field but be able to get that 'feel' to which I have referred, and keep not only up to date, but in line. Buyer/manager can never be an easy job but it holds a fascination, it is difficult to attain, even more difficult to hold, yet few women or men in these posts find it easy to relinquish them in their advancing years.

There is a growing tendency, for economic and other reasons, for departmental stores to have central buying offices, which contribute to the reduction of the buyers' powers and ability to express himself or herself. To explain simply is to over-simplify but, briefly, the theory is that a central buying office can buy in bulk and therefore more cheaply and the goods can be distributed to branches throughout the country. This is true in the case of sheets, blankets, hosiery and in a whole range of everyday merchandise but it has its disadvantages which, in my view, often outweigh the advantages. The practice makes the goods in one shop similar to another and shops become dull. Unless there is something different and better to be found in large stores the shopping public will not travel to town but will shop locally.

A most important point psychologically is that a buyer who has himself selected merchandise is dead keen to sell it, but tends to be critical of goods sent to him from a central office, and above all, the buyer in the store knows his market; tastes differ in every area and central buyers, however good, will never be able to buy fashions, shoes, furniture, soft furnishings, dress fabrics, and so on as successfully as the buyer on the spot, in the store in which the goods are to be sold.

Top management in a good store is unobtrusive, but all staff should be conscious of the fact that it is there. It must control the amount to be spent over a period by each buyer, and have a constant eye on all expenses, including staff wages and salaries. It budgets, or at least it should, in such a way that the business will trade at a profit, but only by constant supervision and a lot of know-how is this achieved.

Stores like to have a 'happy family' image which is often more of a façade than a reality. The chairman likes to be something of a father figure but he is usually as 'tough as old boots' and would 'hang his grandmother'. If he is almost entirely ruthless but lives to a ripe old age, everyone forgets his cruelties and injustices and, in some measure, reveres him as a 'fine old character'. It is curious how, particularly after death, the sins are forgotten and at memorial services one too often has the feeling that someone else is being mourned, for the testimonies to the departed seem to have little bearing on the man that you and everyone else knew. I am not being cynical, merely factual!

The novelist Gilbert Frankau approached me years ago, when he was a little short of cash and thought he could get an advance of £1,000 or so if he could write the history of a departmental store. I tried to dissuade him, as there is a limited interest in stores individually and the juicy bits would be suppressed by the management. Nevertheless he proceeded, but the book was never published. I do not know how true they were, but he told me several bits of scandal relating to a variety of stores that he had unearthed during his research. One well-known store chief was caught in bed with a nearby doctor's wife and it cost him many thousands to have the story hushed up. Another—Frankau told me the name—had, at his death, had as many affiliation orders as there are days in the year. The store chief was a Victorian figure and the employees were pretty well at his mercy. As Churchill is reputed to have said when told of a well-known political figure aged over seventy caught in a compromising situation with a lady of easy virtue on a very frosty night in a London Park, 'Over seventy years of age! Temperature below zero! in the park! Huh! it makes you proud to be an Englishman.'

I know little or nothing of the private lives of the people at top management of stores in my time but have the feeling that the job is so competitive that they are probably too exhausted by the routine of the normal day to compete also with the amorous exploits of their predecessors. But who knows?

People in the fashion world tend to be glamorous and worldly-wise, fun to be with and extremely gifted. We looked for such a one during my management days at the Stores, as it was felt we lagged behind in fashions. Someone came up with the idea that we should employ a fashion co-ordinator and put her over all the fashion buyers. After a long search without success, a young woman came to my office to be interviewed; she had the knowledge, the personality and charm and possessed, I thought, the necessary strength of character. I took a chance and engaged her. She was an immediate success—and soon overcame any opposition from the buyers under her, gaining their co-operation. She was the first to introduce a Mary Quant shop into a department store and rejuvenated all fashion departments—so much so that we put on well over £100,000 that year in fashions alone. Then my boss's son married her and she was lost to the business; this is a hazard in the game. Perhaps that old store chief with all those affiliation orders kept his staff in more senses than one!

I must confess that at one time I rather looked down on departmental stores employees, in particular men connected with the dress fabrics and other 'cissy' departments, but to my surprise, in my capacity as merchandise manager of the Army & Navy Stores, I found myself getting more and more inter-

Thornton's, Broad Street, Oxford: the University booksellers where I served a five-year indentured apprenticeship

A glimpse of the interior of Hatchards in Piccadilly

The charming frontage of Hatchards with the plaque above commemorating the founding of The Royal Horticultural Society there in 1804

ested in the fashion side of the business. The excitement of fashion parades with glamorous models—who, to a fashion buyer, I was told, are little more than clothes pegs and not regarded as women—was new to me and the stage-management of it all I found absolutely fascinating.

I was very much in the background but soon found myself getting more interested in the fashions and indeed, in the techniques, rather than in the models themselves, whom one got used to seeing in various stages of undress. I felt I was becoming sufficiently blasé.

The selling of fashions is a hard, competitive business but with a stimulation of its own and today I have a respect for those connected with it; particularly for the hard-working models, for it is no fun to have to change many times at rehearsal—for everything is timed to a split-second—and again at two and three shows a day. The girls can become positively sore after changing from one tight swim suit to another at speed, but they are real troupers, and it is a pleasure to work with them.

A lively departmental store has a large programme of 'events', all designed to stimulate sales, and no sooner is one over than another has to be stage-managed. It makes for a busy life and a great deal of pressure. Two main sales are held, usually in January and July, followed perhaps by a white sale and special fashion weeks. The January sales have to be planned and organised during the hectic Christmas buying period as they follow immediately after Christmas, and this is often complicated by stocktaking, which usually occurs at the end of January. All this makes for very hard work for the staff as well as management.

Gardening events with perhaps some sort of flower show, wine weeks with tastings, do-it-yourself events linked with the spring season of home decoration, with demonstrators in the store working away with the latest paint rollers, power tools and laminated materials; all these and many more require much correspondence and planning. But unless something is always happening, the store is dull; so it is always necessary to draw people into a store and, once they are there, have something to tempt them to buy.

Hundreds of thousands of people daily spend their lunch breaks in departmental stores, particularly if the weather is bad. With the first spring sunshine these people are tempted for a day or two, especially in London, to go into the parks and eat a picnic luncheon, but whatever the weather they are soon back in the stores, making the luncheon interval the busiest time of the day for the employees and putting a strain on the staffing position because the stores staff, too, must have a luncheon break.

It is often said jokingly that if trade is good the management will preen itself and take all the credit, but if it is bad, it will criticise and blame the buyers. The buyers in turn say the store succeeds in spite of the management who, they believe, have little or no understanding of the particular department for which they buy, and the staff believe they do all the work and those above them are, in the main, parasites. The truth is that top management is the mainspring which sets all the wheels in motion, and without which the business would soon be in difficulties. It is skilled in selecting good buyers and managers and then leaving them, as experts in their own fields, to get on with the job. If management is inefficient it will fail, and the staff will be unhappy and unsettled. Good management must have a deep regard for the staff and make it clear that every member counts.

Staff are of great importance but they are helpless without the capital and experience of those above; so, of course, management and labour are vital to one another and although there is a great deal of leg-pulling and banter, which is all to the good, it is most unusual for a departmental store to have labour troubles. One reason is that staff are too intelligent to be led astray by the lunatic fringe, which seemingly can bring workers in factories out on strike for some trivial reason.

Above all there is a great sense of humour in stores and as people have different jobs with different merchandise, there is always something to talk about and life is never dull. I think too, that the influence of women—and well over fifty per cent of the employees in stores are women—makes life more fun for the men and, I suppose, vice versa, so they are never bored, and it is boredom as much as anything which creates an atmosphere where even a strike is a relief from monotony.

Departmental stores are happy places in which to work and present opportunities for men and women which few outside the retail trade appreciate. It is competitive and something of a jungle at the top, but the financial rewards are good' or even great, and not only I, but all my colleagues started at the bottom. One was a grocer's boy, one an office boy, one a toy salesman, one a display man, but together they all reached the same management board of directors and that is the pattern of top management of most large departmental stores throughout the world.

It must be regarded as a privilege to be in a position of authority in a big concern, conceived and created long before one was born, to play one's part in building up the business, to endeavour to leave it better in every way when, as is inevitable, the time comes to hand over to successors.

Management and buyers of stores travel all over the world to get ideas; one never knows quite what one is looking for and inspirations often come to one from strange sources and experiences. I was holidaying in Rome and learned that pick-pockets could unfasten ladies' handbags with ease and would take money and valuables from them. Most Italian ladies had a double fastener on their bags to frustrate such gentlemen. This gave me an idea, so, with the help of the buyer of the stores' handbag department and a manufacturer, I invented a security handbag which had a lock and key and in addition a zip fastener on each inside pocket. We produced this with a strong double shoulder-strap and had it made in various coloured leathers. It proved to be a great success; we sold thousands of pounds worth over the first year or two and people still want to re-order as their bags get shabby or worn.

Again, I saw abroad for the first time flowered and decorative bathing caps and realised that the old white bathing cap was 'out'. I had some difficulty in persuading buyers that people would, in future, pay as much for a bathing cap as they had been paying for a swim-suit or bikini, so they bought with great caution until they found out that what I had said was right. In Belgium I saw a small counter tray which enabled me to select one small cheroot. With the cigarette smoking scare on I thought more and more people would go over to smoking small cigars, particularly if presented in such a way that they could pick one up for a shilling or less. Many thousands were soon sold and again we were early in the field.

So by observation one gets ideas which earn money and makes the stores' merchandise and its presentation interesting. Other ideas I brought back from the Continent included the now familiar instant shoe repairing bars, first named 'Heel-Bars', and 'Key-cutting while you wait'.

Exotic frozen foods such as Crèpes Suzette and Duck à l'Orange, cheese, and items for the delicatessen counters, all were inspired by Continental trips. Thus it is that London and many provincial stores can provide much of what is best from all over the world, so mitigating in some measure the uniformity of merchandise manufactured at home. Novelty is required even occasionally at the expense of quality. The young lady of today does not, like her mother or, more accurately, her grandmother, necessarily buy quality goods which will last.

Work in a departmental store is not easy in any capacity, the hours are long, the demands of the public exacting, but it *is* living and many prefer it with its hardships and challenges to a humdrum life in small business.

Customers show a great interest in shopkeeping and frequently appear concerned for the welfare of the business. 'Don't you lose a lot of books?' they ask or, 'Surely you must have a lot stolen?' Theft is indeed a serious problem, so it is not unnatural that there is excitement in the catching of thieves. Both staff and management are pleased when a thief is caught—in fact, the capture is frequently due to one of the staff having been particularly 'bright'—but the 'kill' is always a nasty business.

The first time I literally cried when I had to dismiss an employee with many years of service for, of course, not only customers but also staff steal. But one gets over it, though there always remain heart-searchings and a feeling of sorrow. If one becomes too insensitive it is likely one is no longer fit to control a business with a large staff, as heartlessness can express itself in other ways.

Fortunately, there is the lighter side, like the lady to whom was delivered in error one dozen bottles of champagne. When asked to return them, she replied that she had naturally drunk them as she had every right to assume some friend had sent them as a present! Again, there was a case of a lady having five tons of coal shot down her chute in error, (the small iron covers are occasionally near enough to confuse one house with the next). She did not refuse to give it up but insisted that, if we wanted it back, we must get it up the same way as it went in—which was, of course, well-nigh impossible!

Then there was the man who cleared the windows of expensive cigarette lighters. He had the nerve to ask the girl behind the counter for a box to put them in and she gave him one, thinking him to be one of the window-dressers. A man who walked out with a bicycle, saying he was trying it out for size, just rode away. No one questioned two men dressed in white coats who walked out of the store carrying on their shoulders a large carpet, as they were wrongly assumed to be members of the staff just doing their job! It is maddening to be caught by such simple tricks but as people, by and large, are honest, one is off guard.

How much easier life would be if everyone were honest! So many restrictions could be removed. Thieves are an absolute menace to our happiness and welfare; and no one suffers from them more than the shopkeeper.

In my capacities as general manager of the Army & Navy Stores and as manager of book departments in stores and of bookshops, I have naturally been closely concerned with this problem of theft. It was my duty to deal with offenders, and the security measures were also my responsibility. Book thieving, as is well-known, is almost a national disease.

Shop-lifters can be classified into two main categories: first —and they, in my view, are the least worrying—'the professionals' and, secondly, members of the public, both young and old, who deliberately go into shops to steal. Of course, when one of the latter is caught the excuse is, 'I was tempted,' and 'I have never done it before.' They cannot think what came over them, and, if you will let them go free, they will pay for the goods and will swear never to do it again.

Unfortunately experience teaches one that the truth is more likely to be that they have been stealing regularly. In fact, they have been caught because they have done it once too often; and it is quite likely that the thief had, on a previous occasion, taken goods which were missed after he had left the shop, making the sales assistant or manager suspect him because he were last seen behaving in a suspicious manner near the missing merchandise. Assistants are pretty sharp and often remember a face, clothes or peculiarities of people and can identify them.

When goods are missed after a certain shopper has been seen near them, the assistant puts two and two together and is on guard if he returns to have another go. Every shop-lifter, professional or amateur, is a fool, if only because sooner or later the odds are that he will be caught. All professionals have a long list of convictions, as have many amateurs, yet they continue, knowing they will be caught. Most thieves get away with it once or twice but the regular shop-lifter becomes over-confident and will make quite elementary mistakes. The first mistake is to underestimate the intelligence of the sales staff who are ever watchful, although they may appear to be attending to other customers. Assistants know the whereabouts and quantities of stock to a remarkable degree, and the shop-lifter does not take this into consideration. Stolen goods are usually quickly missed.

The thief believes he is a smart fellow, much more alert than the law-abiding citizen, and he is too stupid to learn. He may spend half his life in prison but still has the same delusion.

It is curious that there is much sympathy for the thief and some courts seem to make excuses for shop-lifters. One often reads criticism of shopkeepers for putting temptation in the way of people, by lavish displays, as if temptation justi- fied stealing. How else can a shopkeeper introduce his goods? Taking the attitude of some magistrates to a logical con- clusion, beautiful flower beds in public gardens and parks are a temptation and should be abolished. Private dwellings without iron bars on every ground floor window are a temptation, and so on. There must be a margin of trust in one's approach to the general public.

Shoppers benefit enormously from easy access and open display and life is more pleasant when people are free to look around and see what is new. It is the thieves who make life more difficult than it need be, and cost the country millions of pounds annually, wasting the time of police and the courts. To deprive the shopping public of the pleasure of looking at and handling new merchandise would be retrogressive in- deed; already they have to put up with check-out turnstiles and unwieldy trolleys and wire baskets that catch in other shoppers' clothing, and are obliged to form wearisome queues. All part of the security measures in the new supermarket technique! In many American stores you must deposit large handbags and carrier bags before you enter, so life is full of minor inconveniences made necessary because of the activities of the shop-lifter and the thief. So let's not be sentimental about them.

Book-thieves are a special breed—they include all kinds of cranks, enemies of society, people who have had something stolen from them and want some kind of revenge, 'religious' book lovers who love books but do not wish to pay for them. Some steal to sell, some to possess or give as presents, some for no accountable reason as they do not sell them or read them but accumulate them! Books like umbrellas are borrowed and never returned—so much so that libraries lose vast quantities annually.

Few shop-lifters or book-thieves are so poor that they cannot pay for the goods and, when charged at a police station, they often have considerable sums of money on them. Greed is the simple answer to most amateur shop-lifting. In my experience in departmental stores very many thieves on being caught were found to have stolen other articles from different departments and frequently from other stores and shops. There are legal reasons why the larger concerns always hand the shop-lifter over to the police rather than try to act as judge and jury themselves; but they must be absolutely sure before making any charge or they may find themselves with a claim for very substantial damages for detention or false arrest. The shopkeeper must inform the police of a crime, as it is an offence at law to compound a felony. When all shop-keepers appreciate this and realise that it is their duty to place every case in the hands of the police, then shop-lifting will, in my view, be reduced and magistrates will get a clearer picture of the prevalence of shop-lifting and its cost to the community. At present all too many cases are dealt with by a 'warning' from the shopkeeper, in order to avoid publicity and time-wasting proceedings. Press publicity all too often appears to reflect on the innocent shopkeeper rather than on the thief, whose excuses are plausible and varied.

In one instance a certain reverend gentleman was caught stealing by my house security staff. He had stolen in several departments, so it was not a case of sudden temptation. He was handed over to the police, he admitted the offence, and was later fined. Following the press publicity I had a number of letters from his parishioners, saying we ought to be ashamed as he was such a good Christian gentleman. His story was, according to one correspondent, that he was looking round

Sir William and Lady Collins receiving guests at the first Authors
of the Year Party, 1966

The author (centre) presiding at a Conference of the Booksellers
Association. Left to right: Sir Geoffrey Faber, Sir Basil Blackwell,
Mr Ian Parsons (President of the Publishers Association), Mr
Thomas Joy, Mr 'Gerry' Davies (Director of the Booksellers
Association), Mr Alan Ward (President-Elect of the Booksellers
Association) and Mr Philip Jarvis

The late Enid Blyton autographing books for children

The author talking at a Literary Tea at the Army & Navy Stores, Westminster

the store and had picked up an article which he had intended to buy when the loud-speaker announced that car number so-and-so, which was his car, must be moved, so he dashed to move the car, taking the article with him, and was stopped by a store detective and accused of stealing it. A very good story, but in the first place we had no loud-speaker system in the store, although many stores have; secondly, he had taken a number of articles from a number of departments and had been followed the whole time. The thief is an artist at inventing convincing stories.

Professional thieves make a swoop from time to time on such sections as jewellery, furs, expensive clothes and so on, but their total haul does not add up to a fraction of the losses caused by amateurs, who start stealing as soon as the store is open and continue until it closes. In fact they know that the best opportunities exist at opening and closing times as there is a tendency for some staff to arrive late and to go off early and there are certain duties they have to perform to open up and to close.

The three great worries for retailers are:

1) stealing of stock by the shopping public;
2) stealing of money or stock or both by members of the staff;
3) stealing by professionals.

Sometimes even the shopkeeper appreciates the funny side, although he has suffered loss. For instance, there is the person who tries on a pair of shoes, particularly at sales-time, and walks out with them, leaving the old ones behind. Girls go into dress cubicles to try on a dress or two and walk out having secreted one or more in their clothes. This is stupid as sales staff are trained to count the articles taken into the cubicles and check when the customer leaves. One woman tried to steal a fur coat by secreting it in the rather volumin-ous bloomers she wore for the purpose, but she was a professional and was recognised by the security staff as she left the cubicle.

Not apropos of theft, a rather amusing story, worth telling to illustrate how any form of deceit can lead to complications, is of a well-known lady customer who asked to see fur coats as her husband had recently shown an interest in furs and she concluded he would call to buy her one. As she did not trust his judgment, she had come in advance to select one herself. She asked us to do our best to see her husband bought the one she had chosen, but as hubby almost certainly would not go to the price of 500 guineas, would we say the price was 300 guineas and she herself would pay the difference? The husband came in and asked to see fur coats, and the assistant did her stuff. 'Yes, I am sure it will do nicely,' he said. *'It is a present for my secretary.'* We were in a quandary, as we had under-quoted the price as arranged and how were we to recover the balance? The only way out was to betray his wife by explaining exactly what had been arranged by her. In the circumstances he took it pretty quietly.

Most large stores and multiples have a security staff to catch thieves, both shoppers and staff, so they are the last places where people can hope to steal without being caught. It is true that the staff and the professional thief both get to know the security staff by sight, but there are constant changes and use is made of outside agencies who supply people to check on sales staff and shoppers. No assistant can be sure the person 'shopping' is not 'test shopping' for an agency.

Security staff can be either male or female, but the women are particularly successful as they can disguise themselves by a change of clothing and hair-do. One I knew could look very 'Ascot' one day and like one of the cleaners the next; and she could tackle the strongest man and more than once collected a black eye or bruises in the process.

There is no known one hundred per cent sure system to prevent staff stealing money, instead of paying it into tills or through the cash tube. Whatever the system, loopholes will be found. Test purchases are made, as I have said, by representatives from outside agencies. They come into the shop like ordinary customers and pay cash. Later the records are checked to see whether the correct amount was paid in. They are successful in catching a large number of dishonest sales staff annually.

I have always made it clear to my staff what measures are taken to ensure their honesty as it is not my object to catch thieves but to *prevent* stealing and this, I point out, is in the interests of the staff, as they prosper according to the prosperity of the company. I also make it clear that their personal safety is more precious to me than any goods or cash that thieves may try to steal and they should look after themselves; for instance, if someone is going to bank a large amount of money, he or she should never go alone and it is a good plan to carry an empty brief case with the money in a pocket. By such common sense methods one can often fool the would-be thief.

Staff steal money in a variety of ways, the usual one being by under-ringing. That is to say, they take a pound from a customer and ring up on the till an amount less than the pound, perhaps a shilling or so. They can then extract the difference from the till later and pocket it. Even if they were seen doing this, they would have an excuse, such as, 'I put a pound of my own money in as I was short of change.' Spot checks on tills catch this sort of thief, as if the check reveals that the till is 'over'—that is to say, there is more money in the till than the recorded amount—the assistant is almost certainly up to mischief. But she would be warned at least once or twice before being dismissed for 'incompetence', short of absolute proof.

Waitresses can steal by giving their friends expensive meals and drinks and only charging a fraction of the amount due on the bill. Sales assistants can steal goods by getting friends or relations to shop and then go away with goods for which the assistants have grossly under-charged. The methods are endless, but mostly known to security staff and management. Yet from time to time a new trick is played with success. One of the old tricks which comes up regularly is for someone to go round the store presenting himself to desk cashiers as an official of the company whose job it is to collect the money and take it to the chief cashier's office. At busy seasons such as Christmas or sales time, with temporary staff and extra cash desks, this ruse is often successful, and some cashiers hand over their total takings without question, fearful of disputing the credentials of the collector who just might be someone in authority.

One has no sympathy with the professional thief but, alas, there are often tragedies underlying the stealing of cash by staff. Mostly it is greed, but mental derangement or the dire needs of single women alone in London with high rents to pay—husband possibly having walked out leaving his wife and children—are common reasons and the truth is often pitiful. I, for one, have never ceased to feel upset at being the responsible official to deal with a dismissal and from time to time I will not dismiss. But if one overlooks one offence, where can one draw the line in the next case?

On one or two occasions a member of the staff, nearing pensionable age, has been stupid enough to steal something quite small and of little value, and the punishment of dismissal with loss of pension seemed too severe and unjust to me, so I overlooked the offence. But for all one knows the person may have been stealing over a long period.

A managing director is responsible to his Board and to the shareholders and if any weak policy on his part encourages any form of stealing, he is failing in his duty, so however hard it may be, he must do his job as conscientiously as possible. If a severe warning will do and prove sufficient to get an employee back on the right road to the benefit of the firm, I would advocate it; but there are obvious dangers.

An old joke is to say shopkeeping would be fun were it not for the customers. Yet the old maxim that 'the customer is always right' is still a sound business approach in spite of the fact that the customer is frequently wrong. Of course, the maxim was never intended to be taken quite literally, but if a customer has a complaint, the service has obviously failed to give satisfaction so every effort must be made to regain confidence and retain goodwill.

A few customers are unreasonable and start their day in a bad mood which they take out on others. It takes years of experience in most forms of retailing to be able to answer customers' questions reasonably well and some of the staff have necessarily little experience as, after all, everyone must at some time be a beginner.

I have been threatened during my career by customers— a number being quite important or even famous people— and by cranks and those who enjoy throwing their weight about. They usually complain to one's superiors. For instance if they consider a book is disgusting and one refuses to take it off display and not to sell any more, they frequently bring into their argument the effect reading and selling such a book must have on the younger members of the staff. On this score, at least, they should not worry, as young people in bookshops know the facts of life and can handle them. Some older people know the facts—*but do not like them.*

Sometimes complaints are ludicrous. Not long ago I was asked to remove a harmless thriller displayed in the window because £5 notes protruded from the breast pocket of a uniformed policeman depicted on the jacket and that could lead visitors to this country to conclude that the British police force was corrupt.

In the fruit department an enterprising but naïve assistant put up a notice, 'Tits like coconuts'. This, to his surprise, got him into hot water.

I will not allow my staff to be impolite to customers, however provoked they may be, but some amusing instances have been reported over the years. One lady wrote complaining that a vanman was not obliging and used bad language. She went on: 'As he left my drive I called out to him that I would complain and asked his name. I couldn't quite hear him but it sounded like "Solluks".'

One of the best excuses I heard was from an old assistant in the poultry department, who was reported by a lady for using obscene language. 'Nothing of the sort,' he said. 'All I said was that I was the Duck Plucker.' Staff can be quick to avoid trouble. There was an instance of a customer who called the head waiter and complained that there was a dead cockroach in his food. He may or may not have been right, but this will never be known for the head waiter picked up whatever it was, ate it, and said, 'That was only a chip, Sir.'

In case that story gives a wrong impression of kitchens, I can only say that store kitchens in my experience are left scrupulously clean every night, all the utensils are cleaned and shine with incredible brightness, the benches are scrubbed and the floors washed. Sometimes I have been a bit worried, however, at the food being brought out from refrigerators and returned if not used. I think more instruction on deep-freezing and refrigeration generally is needed by us all in this day and age, and with more knowledge many a stomach upset might be avoided.

To return to bullying or difficult customers, it is at times extremely difficult for staff to judge and make a decision. Let me give an example. A customer may select books or goods he wants to take with him and will offer to pay by cheque. Now, within certain limits, most firms will allow this if the customer writes his name and address on the back of the cheque and—this is the rule—produces some means of identification, such as a banker's card or a driving licence. A few customers will protest strongly at being asked to do this, but they do not appreciate that the loudest protestor of all is the thief with the stolen cheque-book, because he knows he may get away with it if he bullies and frightens the assistant. One cannot always judge by dress or voice but it is nevertheless surprising how often assistants can accurately sum up a customer. One cannot beat the real rogue every time but the public can assist shopkeepers by understanding the need for care even if it means some small inconvenience to themselves.

The whole business of retailing is exacting and nowhere more so than in a large high-class departmental store, but this has the attraction of a challenge.

XII

It is almost impossible for the present generation to appreciate the changes which were brought about during the last century by the creation and development of large departmental stores and of multiple stores. Many of us can clearly remember the days, not so long ago, when there were no supermarkets and recall that they seemed to spring up almost overnight. Quickly they spread all over the country and the shopping habits of this and many other nations changed. The beginnings of the departmental stores were an almost exact parallel, for although the huge departmental stores in London and in the other large cities seem to many of us to have been there forever, in fact they hardly existed just over a century ago.

The introduction of the departmental store was actually begun around 1850 when Bon Marché was created in Paris by a Monsieur Boucicaut. This quickly had far-reaching effects, which have altered many of our ways of life, much more so in fact than the supermarkets in our day.

Boucicaut allowed people to look around, which was a new idea in retailing. He priced everything, whereas before a certain amount of bargaining over price was usual, and he held sales and he delivered purchases. All this idea does not seem very revolutionary today but it was a century ago. Added to this, Boucicaut in his Bon Marché added department after department and created a 'departmental store'. By this the Bon Marché seems to have made the greatest impact on the development of the departmental store but, as with so many 'new' ideas, others were thinking and experimenting along much the same lines rather earlier or simultaneously, both in England and abroad.

Before the departmental store the mass production of good quality clothes at reasonable prices was unknown, because the sales outlets did not exist. Most women with modest incomes had 'a little dressmaker round the corner' and a very large number of men wore only second-hand clothes. Today, with Marks & Spencer and Harrods—dare I bracket these two together?—not only the society girl but the office girl can, in many ways, be better dressed than any princess of past ages. What a transformation there has been even in my lifetime! We look back and laugh at the way we dressed fifty years ago, but at the time we thought we were very 'with it' although that expression was not used.

New fashions have, of course, always been 'shocking' to many. Today's mini-skirts and see-through garments are not by any means the first to bring forth protest from the more puritanical. In my youth girls wore french knickers and, believe me, the stretch tights of today are much more modest. A girl in a punt wearing french knickers was a revelation! Yet, by contrast, 'mixed bathing' was just coming in and considered to be very daring, if not immoral. I recall the first 'bobbed' hair and the first 'marcel' waves which were actually introduced to the general public in Oxford by the father of one of my friends. There had previously been only 'Court' hairdressers, attending exclusively to ladies of fashion. A training scheme was started in Oxford after the 1914-18 war and ladies hairdressing was taught to ex-soldiers as part of a rehabilitation programme. The premises selected were in St Aldates, near the unfashionable area of St Ebbe's. Oxford girls could have their hair waved free if they did not mind being 'guinea-pigs' for learner hairdressers. In fact, if anything went amiss my friend's father—who was a skilled hairdresser—would see that the hair was made presentable before the girl left the premises.

As a boy I hardly ever went into large shops or stores, but the larger stores at Oxford were Elliston's, Badcock's and Webber's. The sister of my first sweetheart was the first mannequin at Elliston's and the display manager of Elliston's —Peter Granville—produced amateur dramatic shows at the Y.M.C.A., in which both my wife and I took part. So began, in a very small way, my contact with stores, which was to lead to my spending thirty years of my life in two of the largest in London and eventually to my becoming Deputy Managing Director of the Army & Navy Stores in Westminster.

My first sweetheart 'Mabs' worked in a small store, Cape's in St Ebbe's, Oxford. I remember the 'Penny Bazaar' there, the forerunners of Woolworth's and British Home Stores, with their trays of pencils, cottons, pins and all kinds of exciting novelties and, later, the opening of Woolworth's in Cornmarket Street. In those days everything on sale at Woolworth's cost either threepence or sixpence. On the opening day of Woolworth's in Oxford almost everyone was seen carrying home the opening bargain, a 'galvanised pail or bowl', price sixpence.

Little did I know that in time to come I would be caught up in retail store business and travel to America, Europe and Scandinavia to study markets and departmental store systems and procedures, and that all of this would, one day, paradoxically make me a better bookseller because business management is much the same, whether one is dealing in books, toys, fishing tackle or wireless sets. The ability to see bookselling in perspective as just one section of the retail trade, proved most useful.

Going back to the days before the departmental store and multiple store, the shopper was largely in the hands of the privately owned business. These were mostly small and one did not always get good value for money before branded merchandise enabled the shopper to know just what he or she was buying. The great advance for shoppers, first introduced by the departmental store, was that they could actually see the goods, handle them, select and even return them if not completely satisfied; thus good value was assured. This was a real breakthrough and, following the enormous success of Bon Marché, departmental stores developed very quickly all over the world; and not surprisingly, America, always quick to see the value of a new trend, was soon in the lead, so that it happens that some of the oldest and finest departmental stores are in America.

This advance in retailing coincided with another move in Britain, the Co-operative Movement, and so it came about that the Civil Service in the Strand was the first departmental store. It opened in 1862 as 'The Post Office Supply Association'. It first supplied Post Office workers who had clubbed together and then later civil servants and their families. A number of officers, both of the Army and of the Navy, wished to enjoy the facilities of the Civil Service Stores and were refused, so in 1872 they set up their own store in an unfashionable cheap property near Victoria Station. It was first called the Army & Navy *Co-operative* Society and sold goods only to the officers of the two services and their wives and families. The store had no shop windows but rather resembled a club, with a good restaurant. It became quite a prestige symbol to be a 'member' of the Army & Navy Stores, and people today boast that their parents or grandparents were original members!

After the First World War, the Stores were declared open to the general public and it trades today much as any other store; but something of the past remains—the wine cellars are still the largest in any retail establishment and deservedly noted as one of the finest—I should know, as I spent quite some time there and had considerable interest in the cellars during my twenty years service with the company! The wine department, not unnaturally, was the first department to open and with a bottle of port at two shillings—no wonder the membership increased. Soon the Army & Navy Stores became one of the largest and best departmental stores in the world, with thousands of employees; selling and manufacturing everything imaginable, from jams to gold watches, pickles to furniture, guns and uniforms, tents and cigarettes and providing every conceivable service from the selling of stocks and shares to the arranging of funerals.

When I was general manager there remained about 100 departments and we had between 1,250 and 1,500 employees. Some of the factories and departments had been closed, many as a result of the war, and were never re-opened because times had changed. The larger manufacturers of branded products—jams, pickles, teas, tobacco, cigarettes, pies and sausages (the list is endless)—were able to cut out the smaller ones and, being geared to a larger output, could be very competitive in price.

Times change: the departmental and multiple stores were largely responsible for marketing, and even causing to be manufactured, a considerable number of branded goods and, as there were insufficient supplies in certain directions to meet their needs, they even produced their own. Now the tables were turned: manufacturers made more and more and so looked for wider outlets. Thus it gradually came about that you could buy a reliable brand locally, making it less necessary to travel to the big store in town.

Behind every assistant seen serving in a departmental store are many more doing every conceivable job from accounts to packing, with outside staff delivering, carpet-laying, furniture removing, decorating, catering, and so on.

Stores are towns in themselves, which make them fascinating places in which to work, with the day-to-day scandal of who is having an affair with whom, births, marriages, deaths, dismissals, newcomers, the jungle of business, the bosses. In management, one can make the day of members of the staff by the right kind word, and good staff relations are tremendously important as the 'image' of the firm is passed on to the customers by the staff who are in constant contact with them. It is no use spending thousands of pounds on advertising how good you are, if the staff tell the public how mean, bad and unbusinesslike the firm is, as compared with the days of the 'old management'. Staff can help make or break any business.

With so many people of differing trades and skills under one roof, from engineers and cleaners to the glamorous fashion models, life can be hard but never dull. If any writer let his imagination run riot, the picture would almost certainly not be as large as true store life, where the episodes, the stories and the tragedies are endless.

Once we found a large quantity of empty bottles which had contained chlorodyne and finally traced an addict on the staff. Again, we found masses of empty sardine, salmon and other tinned food containers at the bottom of a disused lift shaft, the contents of which had been consumed by the staff, but alas! almost certainly not paid for.

I was told of a case, before my time of a display man who was dressing a window as a bedroom setting, and working overtime, persuaded one of his lady assistants to share the bed with him; but they overslept and it was rumoured they were still in bed when the blinds were drawn up in the morning,* to the great interest of the passers-by! One assistant, over-anxious to please, was addressed by a lady who carried an ear trumpet. He was embarrassed and rather confused when the lady said, 'Speak into the trumpet.' Putting his mouth close, he shouted, 'Are you there, Madam?'

At one time we had complaints if a window displayed corsetry, or if a dummy figure was left nude on display. Everything had to be circumspect—so much so, that in one bookshop when a young lady secretary truly fell down the stairs into the arms of the first salesman and the boss arrived at that moment, he was so angry that he actually closed the shop and sent the staff home.

A store is literally filled with Wine, Women and Song, and all these temptations must be resisted, or at least handled discreetly, if one wishes to succeed, for the grape-vine is such that management knows all about what is going on;

* It was at one time customary for shops to draw blinds nightly and over weekends.

and, in turn, even the errand boys know what the management is up to regarding, say overtime pay or Christmas holidays before the senior members of the staff!

Accidents happen frequently, people cut themselves, fall, slip, scald themselves, and so on, so I put a small hospital into the Army & Navy Stores with a State Registered Nurse in full-time attendance. The doctor came at least once a week—and had done so for years before I put in the hospital. I frequently warned the staff of the dangers of standing on the glass tops of show-cases but still some would take a chance and one day an electrician sat on the top of a glass case to attend to the lights on a Christmas tree, the glass gave and blood spurted over the handbags as he had cut an artery. Fortunately he survived but the unfortunate sequel of doubtful humour was that some weeks later a pretty girl assistant showed a little too much interest in the young man replacing this same glass and, stooping to talk to him, nearly cut her nose off on a broken piece. The nose was repaired and only a slight red thread-line was left to remind her of the folly of combining business and pleasure!

It is obviously important to have skilled medical advice where there is a big staff as quick diagnosis—for instance, of a heart attack—can frequently save a life, but equally important it is of enormous help to management to see that the health of the staff and their jobs are not in conflict.

Health and safety, coupled with security of cash and goods, are all part of the problems of management, and they can conflict. For instance, in order to be able to evacuate people quickly in case of fire, doors which would otherwise be closed and locked for security of stock reasons, must be left open. Staff will tie string to handles to keep doors open during the hot weather to get more air, but these are often fire doors which are there for their protection, since if closed they cut off smoke and give the staff time to get to safety. But the main danger is fire from smouldering cigarette ends. Staffs are absolutely reckless with these, showing little concern for their jobs or their safety.

The trouble with a management job is that it must in some measure isolate you from staff and life at the top can be and usually is lonely. So I found it—but of course, it has compensations and hard work is one of them, for contrary to a fairly widespread belief, those at the top work like beavers almost night and day, and can rarely relax and have their minds free from business matters.

The function of good management is there not just to jog along but to create and foster business, to seize opportunities, to inculcate a go-ahead policy; it all sounds easy but in practice it is so exacting that it leads all too often to ulcers and coronaries. There is all too little room at the top, and none at all for weaklings in the retail trades and particularly, in my experience, in departmental stores.

XIII

When I started at the Army & Navy Stores, Westminster (The Stores as it is called by many, dating back to the old membership days) I went from the lap of luxury—for Harrods is indeed a luxurious store, and I had been spoiled there, having been something of a 'blue-eyed boy'—to something very different. My first office at the A. & N. was situated in the rather dirty, gloomy basement. The book-room 'department' was too grand a name, for the stock of books was on the ground floor. This was all that was left of a once magnificent, unrivalled book department. The whole store had suffered in the war years and, to me, not only the book but most departments had an air of neglect compared with what I had been used to.

The Stores had been partly bombed and its trade, particularly its food trade, had suffered severely as a result of food rationing. On top of this a whole floor had been taken over by the Government and used as a factory. This huge area was now empty, awaiting official permission to reincorporate it into the store proper. The staff consisted largely of older personnel, so the vivacity of Harrods seemed to me lacking. Over all, it appeared that there were too many old faithful servants for business efficiency, but as the years passed I learned that many had such skills in their respective crafts, that if once we lost them they could never be replaced.

I, with one other buyer, were the first for many years to be appointed from 'outside', as the policy generally had been

Dame Alicia Markova
between the author
and Mr Peter
Williams (right),
editor of *Dance and
Dancers*

Lord Thomson of
Fleet (centre), Chief
Guest of Honour
at Hatchards' 1970
Authors of the Year
Party, looking at the
display of books with
Mr and Mrs Thomas
Joy. The fabulous
view from the
Martini Terrace (16th
floor of New Zealand
House) can be seen
from the window

The author at the first National Book Sale at the Army & Navy Stores

The late Lord Birkett speaking at the Booksellers Conference banquet during the author's Presidential Year

to promote from within; but we were not at all resented by our new colleagues, in fact we were most warmly welcomed. The Army & Navy Stores has always been a friendly place. Much was expected of us two 'new boys' and fortunately we both succeeded in no small measure. So much so, that in the years that followed, with the book department returned to its former site on the second floor and restored with its fine old bookcases, it became, in my view, second only to Harrods in the departmental stores, and one of the best bookselling retailing outlets in London. It was nice to see people take notice once again when I was introduced at literary parties as the book-buyer for the Army & Navy Stores, as they had once taken notice, when I had been book-buyer for Harrods.

The library which I started at the Army & Navy Stores was a success, and much of this was due to the lucky fact that my secretary at Harrods, Miss Riley, who was also fully qualified in both bookselling and commercial librarianship, joined me; together we built up a first-class and flourishing library service with ever increasing membership.

I arranged Authors' Talks and had large invited audiences to hear and meet such famous people as Somerset Maugham, Chester Wilmot—who wrote *The Struggle for Europe* and who died tragically in a Comet crash shortly afterwards—Sir Basil Liddell Hart, Sir Brian Horrocks, Viscount Auchinleck and many more.

No store I know could compare with the Army & Navy Stores for having so large a percentage of staff who had spent the whole of their working lives at the same store. It was the custom to give a certificate and a cheque to those who completed fifty years service and once I was approached by a man who was still working in the picture-framing department. He was deaf and dumb and about eighty years of age—but through his 'interpreter' he said he had never had a certificate, although he had served over sixty years. He said he would greatly value a certificate but was not asking for the customary cheque. I could not understand how he had been passed by but on investigation found *he was one of the 'temporary staff*'! Needless to say he was given both the certificate and cheque. The explanation of 'temporary' was that in those times such workers were paid, like all factory workers, at so much an hour without holiday pay and were not considered to be on the permanent staff.

Another amusing incident occurred when the management decided to present a gold watch to any member of the staff with twenty-five years service—the later school-leaving age and earlier retirement beginning to minimise the number who could hope to get the former fifty years service cheque. No fewer than 300-odd qualified for watches, so we had a reception with refreshments, with the chairman and directors present. Having seated all the oldest who were to receive the gold watches in the front row, the chairman called the first name on his list. An old man tottered to the platform and began slowly to ascend the few steps. It was such a humorous beginning—almost like a Chaplin film. We began to wonder if he would make it. He did! and the chairman turned to me and said, 'Where does he work?' I confessed I had never seen the man before, but I would ask the staff manager. He too, said he had never seen him before, and so we went down the line and no one seemed to know the man or the nature of his work! Doubtless he had performed some useful function over many years and he certainly got his watch, but it shows how individuals can get lost in a big store!

I managed the book department and the library and, as the years went on, other departments came under my control, including the picture department, music and, later, toys.

One day I was summoned to an interview with the chairman, a rare occasion indeed, and to my surprise, he told me that the directors had decided it was necessary to create a new post, that of merchandise manager. They considered I was most fitted for the job and they would like me to accept it. Would I think it over? I said, 'There is no need for me to think it over. If you have this confidence in me, I accept the challenge.'

My mind was racing as I spoke, because I realised that all

my life in the book trade, with the close contacts that made it my social as well as my business life, would soon in some measure be lost; and just at the time when I was to achieve the highest honour and a lifetime's ambition, the appointment as President of the Booksellers Association of Great Britain and Ireland.

It is a great achievement for any bookseller to become President, but it is obviously easier for someone who personally owns a large business or is the son of the owner of a great bookshop, than for one who started at the bottom and managed not a bookshop but a book department in a departmental store. To start with, there has been over the years no little 'feeling' that store book departments are not comparable with good bookshops, but the facts are that, although there are a number of departmental stores which have only a few annuals at Christmas and little or no book stock throughout the year, Harrods, Selfridge's, the Army & Navy Stores and others in London and the provinces have book departments with representative stock covering a wide field of literature—in some cases rivalling the best and largest bookshops, particularly in general literature and children's books. Obviously booksellers struggling for existence do resent those store book departments which 'cash in' on the Christmas trade, and booksellers—indeed private traders generally— resent the advantages that big businesses, whether departmental or multiple, possess.

It is a tribute to a man if he can, by his personality, knowledge, committee work and general ability, overcome the handicap of being a 'store man'. I would not overemphasise this, because the resentment has become less and less over the last two or three decades; and this is due to the work of people who have held the top positions in book departments in the large stores and in large multiple concerns such as W. H. Smith & Sons Ltd. The whole trade owes much to these people, who have led the way in bringing sections of it together and have done a lot to help the smaller bookseller. It is an indisputable fact that bookshops can now trade at a modest profit and they would not be doing so but for the fact that the larger firms fought for the kind of terms which are necessary for successful retailing.

So, in accepting the post of merchandise manager, I felt I must offer to stand down and not proffer myself at the forthcoming Booksellers Conference for the Presidential Chair. In spite of this, I was duly elected President in 1958 and I had a happy and most successful term of office due to the generosity of the booksellers who elected me, and the officers, members of Council and staff at the Booksellers Headquarters in Buckingham Palace Road who gave me every possible assistance. In particular, the secretary, Gerry Davies, was a tremendous support and a most enthusiastic, utterly reliable friend and colleague.

I had served on almost every important committee of the Booksellers Association over a period of many years and had held many top offices including that of Treasurer, so I was equipped for the Presidency and could accept it with confidence. I think the reproduction of my Presidential Address given in 1958 will give the reader an insight into book trade 'politics' and the importance of the office of President better than any explanation of mine so I reproduce it as an appendix on page 201. I could make the same speech today as things have changed so little in the past years as regards booksellers' problems.

By committee work therefore, I kept in touch with bookselling over the following years and maintained my contacts which served, not only my company but me in good stead, as I was able to come back to 'the Trade' after my retirement from the store world. But I jump my guns.

My whole business life was changed. I no longer would spend a large part of each day with publishers' representatives, examining the new books and promoting the sales of those I judged to be outstanding. I would no longer have a close personal contact with a small staff, which always meant much to me, but instead I would be responsible for a staff of well over one thousand and stock worth over a million pounds.

As this was a new post I had no background, just an office with an empty filing cabinet, but I had two great chiefs. First was the now late Chairman, Commander Lyttelton, a man of the highest integrity, with a love of humanity and a great leader. Then came James Williamson, who had had a meteoric career at the Stores, progressing from a small family business in the Isle of Man to a position of buyer and then to managing director of the Army & Navy Stores branches in India, Calcutta, Bombay and New Delhi. He had returned to England after the war, when the Indian branches were closed. He was appointed general manager of the Stores in Victoria Street and was later promoted to managing director.

As his second in command I was able to learn a lot from him and particularly during my first year in top management. I was always interested in sales promotion and he encouraged me in the 'events' I arranged; exhibitions of all kinds, window displays, authors' talks, cookery demonstrations, fashion parades and so on, all of which brought customers into the Stores and increased business.

One of the most interesting 'events' I arranged, assisted by my friend and colleague Roy Davidson, was a Ballet Exhibition, which ran for a month, during which time famous ballerinas and choreographers appeared in person and the exhibition of memorabilia connected with the ballet personalities was unique. Stars like Markova and Beryl Grey came and gave talks accompanied by members of the corps de ballet.

As a contrast I also arranged an exhibition for Remploy and had some of the handicapped people actually in the Stores working the machines on which they were normally employed.

An event linked with the publication of a book on salads written by Bebe Daniels brought her to the Stores with Ben Lyon and their family. We also had 'The Archers'—complete with signature tune on a gramophone record! This was very popular. Such events were highlights, coupled with the organisation of the usual seasonal sales and the special Christmas attractions.

I was promoted to assistant general manager and later to assistant managing director with the responsibility of running the whole Store in Victoria Street, Westminster; a fascinating but exacting post. The company was now expanding and purchased first Harvey's in Guildford, then Genge's of Dorchester, Green's of St Albans and others, and as this expansion took the chairman and managing director away a good deal of the time, I was often alone in charge.

We had, over the years, 'traded up'. That is to say we were interested in having only high-quality goods and services and it is still my belief that there will always be a demand for the best, and all too few places remain where the best is to be obtained. The policy was in my view successful, and I would not change it were I still in management of the Stores.

I had always intended 'retiring' from store life early and had made this clear, as I think too many people go on too long; some have long passed their best before they reach retirement age and I did not want this to happen to me. Yet I believe nothing is as valuable as experience. After all with whom would you rather invest money—with older folk who have proved successful over a period of years or with untried, comparative beginners? There is much to be said for the untutored wisdom of primitive tribes who invariably leave important decisions in the hands of the elders.

I have made this point because, particularly since the last war, this country, more than others I believe, has become age-conscious to an absurd degree! Older people can be valuable too. Churchill did not do too badly after he was sixty years of age, Somerset Maugham, J. B. Priestley and a whole host of creative artists excelled as they grew older. The list is endless of successful elderly statesmen, inventors, judges, business tycoons—in fact age is rarely a handicap in any walk of life except sport and flying and activities where physical requirements at top level are vital. In intellectual fields and where industry coupled with know-how are important, the older man or woman may do better.

Be that as it may, the time came when I was offered early retirement on pension and I accepted this with mixed feelings. It is certainly nice to be financially independent and to be in a position to take things easy particularly if one has never been in that happy position before, but as far as I was concerned this was 'not on'. I *needed* to have the challenge of the day-to-day difficulties of business with all its economic and staffing problems. I did not want to miss the pleasure of meeting people, and the satisfaction of making a contribution to the progress of a firm and, I hoped, indirectly to that of my country; so I could not retire altogether from business and had never really intended to do so. Although, as I say my feelings were mixed, I was not altogether sorry to retire from 'big business' which was becoming more of a jungle. I am inclined to the view that every big business man should have a sabbatical or at least six months holiday every five years, as he needs the rest not only for health reasons but to keep his perspective right. But it is an old adage that 'change is as good as a rest'. I decided on change.

It is not surprising that after so many years in the business I was still at heart a bookseller and fortunately I could return to the trade: a trade where we are all friends, even with our nearest rivals, and a trade in which we are ever ready to help one another. 'Booksellers,' indeed, 'are generous, liberal-minded men.' So it was in Samuel Johnson's day—so it is today.

I was offered a manager's position by Bob (Robert) Maxwell at Oxford, under my old chief, Cadness Page from Harrods, who too had just retired and taken up a post linked with the Pergamon Press. But as both my wife and I had lost our parents, who had lived in Oxford all their lives, we did not feel we wanted to return, at any rate not yet. So I looked for a challenging job in London, and was indeed fortunate that the one post I particularly wanted was available to me, that of managing director at Hatchards.

It seems I was fated to work at Hatchards. I believe in fate!

But I was indeed fortunate in having such a wonderful opportunity. I intended to make the most of it and prove, if I could, that sound business experience in a large concern could make a better bookseller than bookshop experience alone. The importance of skilled management in retailing is today more appreciated and the book trade is no exception. Large bookshops need skilled management to a degree previously unnecessary, so it would be interesting to put into effect the results of my years of management training and experience and, at the same time, a very worth-while endeavour, for better bookselling had become something of a religion with me.

Sir Alan Herbert and Agatha Christie (Lady Mallowan), both celebrating their 80th birthdays, cutting the tape at the official opening of a new branch of Hatchards at Harvey Nichols on October 2nd, 1970. On the left is the writer, Jilly Cooper

'Autographing sessions are part of a bookseller's life'—Lady Bird Johnson, wife of the former U.S. President, is seen here signing copies of *A White House Diary* at Hatchards on November 27th, 1970, with the author (left) and Mr R. D. Woods, Central London representative of Weidenfeld & Nicolson (Photo by courtesy of Mark Gerson (Photography) Ltd)

(*Left*) 'I love travelling abroad'—self, with pipe, wife on camel, in Morocco

(*Middle*) 'I caught my first shark, a small one'—we let the big one get away! (Bermuda)

(*Below*) Cruising on the Thames with my wife

XIV

The history of a famous and old-established bookshop is in itself a social study: particularly is this true of Hatchards in Piccadilly. It was established in 1797 and flourishes today as not only 'the world's finest bookshop' but as the only remaining bookshop on the grand scale with such early beginnings in London.

Hatchards carries a stock of books worth well over £150,000, a staff of seventy-five people and has an international reputation. Books are sent daily to every part of the world. It is hardly surprising that as managing director, I am somewhat envied—but then booksellers are generally envied, as bookselling is regarded as an occupation for gentlemen. Booksellers, it has been said, 'are seldom rich, they become placid and stoical, their philosophy resting on a love of books and of people who write and buy them'. For my part it is only human to feel proud to follow such great booksellers as John Hatchard and his successors and, in the light of their greatness and of the history of the business, one must, like Uriah Heep, feel 'the 'umblest person going'.

John Hatchard, the founder of the business, was a remarkable man. After serving an apprenticeship of seven years with a Mr Ginger, who had a small bookselling and publishing business in Westminster—Ginger's bookshop sold books to Westminster School and to the Royal Society, but little more is known of it—he followed on as a shopman with a famous bookseller, Tom Paine, 'Honest Tom', whose shop was in

Mews Gate—a site now occupied by the National Gallery. Of 'Honest Tom' it is said he was 'warm in his friendships as in his politics, a convivial companion and unalterable in the cut and colour of his coat, uniformly he pursued one object, fair dealing!' John Hatchard worked for Paine for seven years and eight months before opening his own bookshop in Piccadilly in 1797 with a capital of as little as five pounds.

It is interesting to note the similarity of my early years in bookselling and John Hatchard's beginnings. I too, was bound as an indentured apprentice, in my case for a period of five years, and afterwards I worked in various departments and in various capacities for a period of another ten years before I took the plunge and aimed for management. He started out at fourteen years of age, which was then the usual age for apprentices. In Oxford there were still apprenticeships under indenture as late as the 1920s just as there had been when John Hatchard started out in 1782.

John Hatchard wrote in his diary, 'When I commenced business I had of my own a property of less than five pound but God blessed my industry and good men encouraged it.' He died on June 21st, 1849, and the annual turnover of the business was by then the fantastic sum of half a million pounds.

His memorial tablet in St Paul's Church in Clapham reads:

> In memory of John Hatchard of Clapham
>   Common Esqre.
> Bookseller and Publisher in Piccadilly
> Steadfast in the grace of Our Lord Jesus
>   Christ in the love of God The Father
>   and in the Communion of The Holy
>   Spirit.
> He shewed forth the fruits of his faith in
>   works of benevolence to men.
> He departed this life June 21st, 1849
>   Aged 80 years

but his true 'memorial' is the beautiful bookshop in Piccadilly.

Hatchard was one of the first booksellers to go west, as up to this time the great bookshops were in the City of London, from Elizabethan days in or near St Paul's Cathedral and Churchyard, and the West End was still largely undeveloped. Piccadilly was described as 'the most magnificent street in London, radiant with gleams of brilliance and unexpected light'; but it was in fact, dimly lit by gas, the newest form of lighting. Heavy waggons rumbled slowly past the old wall in front of Burlington House on their journeys westwards and sometimes the peace of the illustrious occupants of Albany Chambers would be disturbed by the cry of 'Stop thief', when a post-chaise was attacked by a highwayman in Piccadilly.

The move from the City began with the Great Plague in 1665 and the Great Fire of London the following year. Many booksellers lost their businesses and were ruined. Book-selling moved to Paternoster Row, but the move westwards to the Strand and the end of Fleet Street began. Dodsley, the poet, opened a shop in Pall Mall in 1735.

Hatchard's new shop was a meeting place for Evangelicals and Tories. Hatchard in his early days in Piccadilly published *Reform or Ruin: Take your Choice*, by John Bowdler. This John Bowdler was the father of Thomas Bowdler who removed sex from Shakespeare and added the word 'bowdler-ize' to the English language. Wilberforce with The Society for the Bettering of the Conditions of the Poor held meetings at Hatchards.

Here, in 1804, was held the inaugural meeting of the Royal Horticultural Society. Here, too, was formed an amusing Society 'to promote marriage'—the forerunner of the modern marriage bureau, with the object of promoting matches and convening meetings for enquiring into the suitability of the contracting parties or supplying information to members which would help them to make their choice.

John Hatchard also held a unique position among philan-thropists; he saw to it that subscriptions to charities were collected at Hatchards—for example, it is chronicled that after the Battle of Waterloo contributions for the 'Waterloo Subscription' were received by 'Mr' Hatchard—and when he died at the age of eighty he left a number of legacies in his will.

In appearance John Hatchard was the very essence of respectability, dressing in a semi-clerical style as befitted his distinguished clientèle which read—as it still does—like an extract from *Who's Who* or *Debrett*. Early patrons included Lord Byron, who lived in Albany opposite Hatchards, as also did Thackeray and Macaulay, where the latter wrote a great part of his History. Both frequented Hatchards. William Wilberforce not only held meetings at the bookshop but had his letters addressed there. Mr Gladstone was a frequent visitor, the Duke of Wellington came on horseback, and Lord Palmerston, Sir Robert Peel and celebrities from all walks of life shopped there.

For many years the Hatchard family occupied part of the house at 187 Piccadilly and the shop itself, lit only by oil lamps, had something of the atmosphere of the old literary coffee house, which had by this time fallen out of vogue, and was frequented by the most famous personages of the day. The daily papers were laid out on a table by the beautiful fireplace—which still remains—and there they sat, in old-fashioned chairs, making a pretence of reading, and dozing off at odd moments when they had exhausted their favourite topic of discussion. Outside the shop was a bench to accommodate the flunkeys who rode behind their masters' carriages.

The term 'bookseller' in Hatchard's day meant in most instances 'publisher and bookseller' and John Hatchard was no exception. He published political and moral tracts and many important books—the best known being *Tupper's Proverbial Philosophy*—a piece of good old Victorian piety but a best-seller in its day and made both the author and John Hatchard £10,000 each.

In 1893 a customer appeared with an unusual request. The customer was Cecil Rhodes, who had arrived from the Cape, enthused by a late reading of Gibbon's *Decline and Fall of the Roman Empire*. He demanded from Hatchards a copy of every authority cited by Gibbon in writing his mammoth history. Research showed that many of the works consulted by Gibbon had never been translated from the Latin or Greek. 'Get them translated,' he demanded, and Hatchards had in effect, practically a blank cheque. Scholars were hired and set to work; the task was enormous and was never, for various reasons completed, but scores of new translations were made and a most valuable library collected, which is priceless today and is housed in the Rhodes Library at Groote Schuur.

For all its staid traditions, bookselling is full of surprises —sometimes provided by the trade itself. In 1918 Hatchards shocked many of its customers by giving a full window display to a book that shattered many conceptions of woman's sexual role—its title *Married Love* by Marie Stopes. I knew Marie Stopes and sat next to her at a Foyles Luncheon about six months before her death. I told her how much I admired her and that she should write her autobiography as few people today realised how persecuted and hounded she had been when she had first advocated and taught birth control. She said that she felt that she had plenty of time in the years ahead to do it but, alas, it was not so.

Bookselling has often to anticipate public taste if it is to survive. It has also to be organised on modern efficient lines to meet new demands.

Today, with its own modern methods in an old-world atmosphere, Hatchards maintains a skilful blending of ancient and modern, which not every old-established business has been able to achieve.

Since the time of Queen Charlotte, wife of George III, Hatchards have been booksellers to members of the Royal Household. The Duke of Windsor (when Prince of Wales), the late Duke of Kent and the Duke of Gloucester were all customers and, as children, Her Majesty, The Queen and her sister, H.R.H. Princess Margaret paid Christmas visits to the shop, as did their grandmother, the late Queen Mary. Today Hatchards are the proud holders of three Royal Warrants—for Her Majesty, The Queen, H.R.H. The Duke of Edinburgh, and Her Majesty Queen Elizabeth, The Queen Mother—and I have had the privilege of attending to the book requirements of the Royal Family over many years.

Hatchard left the large sum of £100,000 at his death—a very large amount indeed in 1849—and, in my view, he made the greater part of this in publishing rather than in bookselling. In Hatchards's archives are a number of interesting documents with an impressive list of customers: the Duke of Richmond, the Duke of Leeds, Lord Clancarty and Lord Saye and Sele, Lord Bolton, and Bishops including Sarum, Winton, Chester, Oxford and several more. In the visitors' book are the signatures of those serving with Nelson at Trafalgar, beginning with Cockburn, (Sir George Cockburn, Admiral of the Fleet). It would appear likely that there was a reunion of Nelson's officers at Hatchards some years after Trafalgar. Many signatories added a note: Robert Drummond, for example, adds, 'Servant to Lord Nelson in *Victory*.' Thos. Bennett, Capt. Ret. adds, 'Late Midshipman of the *Victory* promoted by Lord Nelson from Amphian in 1803 before his Lordship removed his Flag to the *Victory*.'

Macaulay had books from Hatchards from boyhood and in my office I have an illuminated extract from Trevelyan's *Life of Macaulay* which reads, 'You must go to Hatchards and choose another book. I think we have nearly exhausted the Epics. What say you to a little good prose? Johnson's "Hebrides" or Walton's "Lives"...' The letter goes on, 'Or would you like a neat edition of Cowper's "Poems" or "Paradise Lost"?' This letter was written by Hannah Moore to Macaulay when he was eight years old.

John Hatchard was succeeded by his son, Thomas Hatchard. Thomas was not the eldest son but the second son. The eldest—also named John—went both to Oxford and Cambridge and became a vicar in Plymouth. Thomas Hatchard managed the business until his death in 1858—less than ten years after the death of his father—and that was the end of the Hatchard family in management.

As in the case of most booksellers/publishers, the publishing side very slowly disappeared. This is curious, since they might have done better as publishers as bookselling was to face very difficult times.

Mr A. L. Humphreys, who became a famous bookseller and was in the trade for over fifty years, started at Hatchards in 1881. The firm had lost a considerable amount of money over a girls' magazine *Atalanta* and was offered for sale in *The Times* in March 1891. Edwin A. M. Shepherd, the manager at the time, bought the business and took A. L. Humphreys into partnership.

The firm did well under this management and also had the good fortune of supplying the Rhodes Library to which I have referred. Hatchards had this extra business until the death of Cecil Rhodes.

Hall Caine, Rudyard Kipling, George Moore, Andrew Lang, Robert Hichens, Anthony Hope, G. K. Chesterton, John Galsworthy and Somerset Maugham all came to Hatchards with their friends, either as authors or customers, usually both. Oscar Wilde visited the bookshop regularly, coming for the last time on the eve of the production of *The Importance of Being Earnest*. He entered with Lord Alfred Douglas to buy a translation of Aristotle's *Poetics*. In the more recent past callers have included such figures as Lloyd George and Lord Birkenhead, and today it is Edward Heath, walking across from Albany,* J. B. Priestley, Virginia Cowles and many others.

At one time the old shop front was 'modernised' and two large plate glass windows were put in, but the old front with its bow windows was restored in 1908 and remains to this day.

Bookselling during the war years was in certain respects easy. There were, of course, considerable problems, particularly that of staff shortage, as the experienced staff joined

* A few days after writing this Mr Heath became Prime Minister and moved to Number 10 Downing Street.

the forces and had to be replaced by less skilled labour, but as books were scarce and far fewer titles published—in fact only one fifth of the number now published annually—it was easier to deal with such reduced supplies than with normal output.

Booksellers could sell practically any book they could get from the publishers, but paper was rationed, and as a consequence publishers were forced to ration supplies of books to booksellers, as they could not print enough copies of each title to meet the demand.

As the war years passed fewer and fewer new titles were published, which allowed more copies of each to be printed. Most booksellers began to order more copies than they expected to get, as they knew they would receive a small percentage of the total ordered. Some of us who in peace time would have ordered anything from a hundred to a thousand copies of a title now ordered a thousand copies where we would have ordered a hundred and thousands where we would have ordered one thousand, knowing we were unlikely even to get the total we would have had pre-war. Similarly smaller booksellers ordered a hundred copies hoping to get a dozen or so.

This was found to be necessary in some measure as some publishers were not particularly business-like and instead of allocating as fairly as possible on a pre-war demand basis they found it easier to apply a system of scaling down orders on a mathematical basis. By simply dividing the number of copies printed into the total ordered they made their allocations, which resulted in larger and larger orders being placed by booksellers.

The demand for books had increased enormously for a variety of reasons. The blackout resulted in long evenings with little to do; newspapers and periodicals were very small and soon read. Troops were situated in remote areas and wanted something to occupy their minds; prisoners of war wanted books. People on active service and those engaged in fire-watching and other civil defence organisations had all too many boring hours off or on duty, which books relieved. So books brought consolation, entertainment and education, but only in part could the demand be met.

The situation changed with the declaration of peace, and booksellers were caught by having continued too long the 'over-ordering system', although paper rationing continued long after the cessation of hostilities. Few people in the trade realised that the change would be dramatic. By 1949 the situation was serious; on top of this problem of too much stock there were other problems. Booksellers who had joined the forces were often well-trained and potential future managers but, for various reasons many did not return to bookselling. This loss of personnel left a gap which is felt to the present day, for not only was there the loss of people who did not return but five years or so of training had also been lost, and bookselling is a trade in which continuity is all important. It simply is not possible to make up lost time in bookselling; even after two weeks holiday, assistants confess to being lost for a while.

Most important, the world had changed and business had to change quickly to meet the new challenges. Not only bookselling but retailing generally had to adapt itself to the times or close up shop, as rents, rates, light, heat, telephones, stationery and wages were sky-rocketing. To keep in business modern methods and better management were needed, but not all booksellers could meet this post-war challenge. Like the dodo they just could not change, so, finding it impossible to make ends meet, they had to sell out or close their shops. Alas! a number of quite famous booksellers—many London landmarks—have closed in recent years.

Hatchards had its share of troubles. It changed hands several times and had a succession of managers. It was not doing well—so badly in fact that there was a real danger that with its high Piccadilly overheads, it might go out of business, so the fine old bookshop might well have become a restaurant or coffee bar. It was saved by 'Billy' Collins (Sir William Collins Kt., C.B.E., Chairman of William Collins,

Sons & Co. Ltd.) who felt strongly that Hatchards must be preserved as a bookshop whatever the cost. He persuaded Teddy Cole, manager of the business and one of a group of financiers who jointly owned it, to sell Hatchards to Collins to ensure its continuance as a bookshop and it was acquired by William Collins Sons & Co. in the year 1956.

From that date, Hatchards has gone from strength to strength, as the business needed the injection of capital as well as more skilled and experienced management. By a coincidence Teddy Cole had himself tentatively, about that time, offered Hatchards to me, saying kindly, 'You are the only one I know competent to manage it.' Teddy Cole had a genuine love for the bookshop, I was then in an important position at the Army & Navy Stores and although not exactly at pensionable age, I was, in my judgment, too near it to accept his very generous offer. Strange how it was destined that I should, in due course, manage Hatchards after all.

'Billy' Collins has had phenomenal success as a publisher and in considerable measure this is doubtless due to his knowledge of bookshops all over the world and to his intense interest in them. For my part I was fortunate in being available at the right time to be appointed managing director.

What is of special interest is that the great publishing house of Collins with its offices in St James's Place, London, has many parallels with Hatchards. Today the truly fantastic printing works and bindery in Glasgow, which employs thousands of people and which turns out some thirty-five million books a year, over a million Bibles and over eight million diaries, is a far cry from its humble beginnings. Yet both Collins and Hatchards had humble beginnings and subsequent phenomenal success. It is remarkable that the two firms, far apart geographically, had a very considerable measure of overlapping of interests in their early years. So much so that names which influenced Hatchard crop up time and again in Collins history, for instance, Wilberforce, the Duke of Wellington, Lord Melbourne, Sir Robert Peel.

The first William Collins was, like John Hatchard, a

remarkable man, and they had much in common. Collins started publishing in 1789. John Hatchard opened his bookshop in 1797. Both had high moral principles, both published religious books and books on social problems and both were connected with the Evangelical movement, 'which had given Britain a new conscience'.

The union of Hatchards with Collins in 1956 was therefore particularly apt, and here is another instance of history repeating itself, because by the amalgamation both bookselling and publishing are again performed by one company, Hatchards being booksellers only, but also a subsidiary of Collins publishing. I think no one would dispute that 'Billy' Collins, Chairman of both Hatchards and Collins, is the last of the 'giant' personalities of publishing. He was knighted in the Birthday Honours List, June 1970, and everyone in the trade rejoiced.

Sir 'Billy' is a veritable dynamo of a man, who is always to the fore in promoting anything good for the trade and the people in it. He loves Hatchards, so much so that I call it his 'yacht'. He, as the owner as it were, indicates the destination; it is my job as 'skipper' to steer it there safely. His top priority is that nothing should stand in the way of Hatchards being the best bookshop in the world and he expects a service to justify this claim. The making of profit is secondary to this, but obviously it is my job to achieve both aims.

A major structural alteration was made in Hatchards in 1965, which has resulted in substantially increased business. The most important part of the change was the introduction of a strikingly new, handsome, 'late Georgian' staircase. Michael Lloyd was asked by 'Billy' Collins to bring the second floor into focus, to improve the lighting and to bring things up-to-date, while retaining the aura of Hatchards. This was accomplished to the satisfaction of customers, management and staff and resulted, among other things in a fine, improved antiquarian book department on the second floor, a larger art book gallery which contains almost every good British art book in print and many from abroad, and a new, enlarged, most comprehensive paperback department.

The mail order trade has grown enormously in the past ten years or so and thousands of books are posted daily to private individuals all over the world, particularly in America.

John Hatchard would, I feel, be as proud of Hatchards today as he doubtless was in his life-time and the saving of Hatchards by 'Billy' Collins, although only one of his many achievements in a long and distinguished career, is the one, I feel sure, nearest to his heart. Few would deny that the preservation of Hatchards—this 'landmark' in British book-selling—is of no little national importance, since it is a bookshop loved and esteemed by visitors to London from home and abroad. Hatchards is part of our heritage and any one who has contributed to its success both in the past and in the present will have made at least some impression on our cultural life.

Hatchards' 'Authors of the Year' Party is regarded by many as the literary party of the year. It is a grand affair, to which all authors of the year's best-sellers are invited, together with their respective publishers. So each year the party is a glittering assembly of writing talent; but it is more than this, because the party is augmented with prominent people in other walks of life—Ministers, politicians, stage, screen and TV stars, sportsmen etc.

The guest list is obviously different each year, depending as it does on top sales of individual authors. It reads like an extract from *Who's Who*. Personalities as varied as Harold Macmillan, Lord George-Brown, the late Lady Violet Bonham Carter (Baroness Asquith of Yarnbury), Enoch Powell, Lord Thomson of Fleet, the Duke and Duchess of Bedford, David Frost, Sir Alan Herbert, Sir Steven Runciman, Sir William Collins, Sir Arthur Bryant, Sarah Churchill, Michael Denison and Dulcie Gray, Jack de Manio and Moira Shearer have attended, to lend extra charm and interest to the evenings.

Authors are invited on the basis that, if they have published books that year that have subsequently appeared in the lists of best-selling books published by such papers as the *Sunday Times*, the *Evening Standard*, the *Evening News, Smith's Trade News*, etc., then they would usually receive an invitation. These lists of best-sellers are based on information obtained from booksellers all over the country and are, in my view, usually accurate.

A few authors, like Sir Arthur Bryant, Dennis Wheatley and Agatha Christie, top the best-seller lists almost annually; other leading authors, like Iris Murdoch, Margaret Drabble, Georgette Heyer, Jean Plaidy, Margaret Lane, Hammond Innes and Laurie Lee, publish less frequently, so that there is plenty of change at each party.

Exciting guests, who are particularly welcome, are those who have written autobiographically of their special achievements. Recently these have included Sir Francis Chichester, Sir Alec Rose and Robin Knox-Johnston.

I arranged the first party in 1966 and it came about this way. As a bookseller I wanted to express thanks to the best-selling authors, for it is they who help booksellers to remain in business, and one morning I awoke with the vague idea of inviting *all* the best-selling authors of that particular year to a party, which would bring together writers from all kinds of literary fields. I felt sure that they would enjoy meeting one another and exchanging ideas in a pleasant, social setting. Many good ideas have small beginnings. I had, as I say, at the back of my mind this germ of an idea but it did not take shape until after a casual conversation which I had with the Martini public relations officer, now my good friend, Dennis Grahame. In our chat, I talked about authors' signing parties and other events I had arranged and hoped to arrange for Hatchards, and Dennis made suggestions which crystallised into the first Authors of the Year Party and to its being held at the Martini Terrace, which is on the sixteenth floor of New Zealand House in London's Haymarket. This terrace has surely the most impressive panoramic view of London. I arrange the parties in the spring, so as to enable the guests to see this beautiful view, first in daylight and then as dusk falls, so that as the lights come on gradually, you have spread before you London by night! The sight is unforgettable.

Almost immediately the party was established, it became a great success and, as I hoped it would be, something of a prestige symbol. To be invited is, in itself, regarded by writers as a mark of success; some authors of distinction are not necessarily best-sellers, so a selection of these is invited each year.

Hatchards' invitations gave particular pleasure to the Rev. Keble Martin, when he had finished his fantastic best-seller, *A Concise History of British Flora*. This book was the result of his life's work but it was not until he was eighty-eight years of age that he saw it published. This delightful man was the 'star' of the evening at the 1966 party and he wrote about the pleasure it afforded him in his autobiography *Over the Hills*.

At the first party there were some 200 distinguished guests, including thirty-two best-selling writers of 1965. This function was televised, which was good publicity not only for Hatchards but, even more so, for the authors. The most recent party, in the spring of 1970, was commented on in Jack de Manio's radio programme, 'Today', and some of the authors present were interviewed.

So each year's party seems better than the last one and brings, one hopes, extra prestige to writers, extra publicity and extra sales of their books. A bookseller is doing his job if he promotes authors and the sales of their books, and Hatchards' Authors of the Year Party does just that. Of course, both Hatchards and I are indebted to the Martini Club for their hospitality, for the success of the party undoubtedly depends to a great extent on its being held on their magnificent terrace, and I am grateful to Dennis Grahame for his inspiration.

There was a time when poets, playwrights and novelists were lionised, like the film stars and pop singers of today. Hostesses clamoured for them to come to their parties; they made news not only by their writings but by the details of their everyday lives, which were exposed and discussed.

Dickens, Marie Corelli, Wilde, Ouida, and many others regularly made news headlines, were lionised and sometimes ostracised.

The cultural salon has almost died out in this country, which is a pity. Writers today are, instead, interviewed on TV and radio, but this does not bring them into personal contact with their contemporaries as did the salon or the old Bookshop Coffee House. I cannot help thinking what tremendous impact some of the old authors would have made on TV. Imagine readings by Charles Dickens! He loved an audience and travelled all over the country to give readings of his books. I possess a copy of the special version of *A Christmas Carol* which he used. It was reduced, to allow him to tell the whole story in one evening. Oscar Wilde, too, loved an audience and would doubtless have made piquant replies to any TV interviewer.

The age produces the men, so, with the advent of new media, it is not surprising that there are few public literary figures today. Even so, Britain is fortunate in having many great writers; but neither they nor their books receive sufficient publicity. I am proud to be able to acknowledge the debt we owe them with Hatchards' Authors of the Year parties.

XV

As a businessman, I am firmly of the opinion that plenty of holidays are good, not only for physical reasons but because the unwinding process is vital to people who tend to over-work. On occasions I have saved colleagues and staff from jeopardising their careers simply by spotting that they needed a good holiday. The more reluctant they were to take one, the more essential and beneficial it proved to be.

Oxford is a long way from the sea, in fact it is just about as far away from the coast as any town in England, so it is not surprising that with a family of seven children my parents did not take us on long train journeys for seaside holidays but took riverside bungalows. I was in my early teens before I had a few days at the seaside; and had never seen the sea excepting for a vague childhood memory of being with my mother on a cliff looking down on a beach and watching a black-faced comedian performing on a platform. We were eating a sausage with a red skin—a poloney or saveloy—and I buried my head in Mother's lap, as I was frightened by the black-faced comedian.

Apparently I was taken to Ramsgate when I was between two and three years old and years later I was able to verify that there was a famous black-faced comedian there at that time and ultimately, some thirty years later, when I revisited Ramsgate, the setting was exactly as I had remembered it from the early visit.

My first visit to the seaside, excluding this babyhood excursion, came about when visiting my uncle and aunt who lived in Crewe. They decided to take a trip, which they frequently did, to Colwyn Bay and to stay there for a few days, and luckily they wanted to take me as company for their only son, Leonard. I cannot describe the thrill and all it meant to me to be going to the seaside for the first time and, what is more, *by car*. Few people possessed cars in those days, but my uncle had a uniformed chauffeur and a luxury car called a Delawney Bellevue. I am not certain of the spelling, but it sounded wonderfully plutocratic. It was an exciting journey. We had no fewer than seven punctures on the way. Neither the roads in Wales nor motor tyres were of today's standards, so it was usual to carry many spare inner tubes as well as the spare wheel. We needed all we carried to get us to Colwyn Bay that day.

My first view of the bay took my breath away and I have never got over the sight of the enormous rounded boulders like huge pebbles gradually decreasing in size down to small ones near the shore. In the morning sunlight they were vivid blues and whites. The sandy shore was covered with thousands of starfish, some as large as side plates, some quite small, some almost golden in colour and others various shades of red, pink and brown. Whether some freak storm had brought them ashore or whether this phenomenon happens each year, I do not know, but I have never seen anything like it at any time anywhere else.

It was, I recall, stormy weather; on my way down to the beach the cable for the electric tram was struck by lightning almost in front of me. It was not frightening, since it produced little more to see than the blowing of a large fuse. I have revisited Colwyn Bay from time to time over the years but the magic of that first morning was never recaptured and the pebbles do not seem to have the delicate hues I saw then; but it is still beautiful. The great surprise was that the surf made a noise! I had seen the waves rolling into the shore many times at the cinema—silent of course—and never appreciated that the breaking of the waves over the shingle would be noisy.

In my early years at work I could not save much to travel far. One of my first holidays as a young man of seventeen or eighteen was to Brighton. I went with my friend Charles, who was very handsome, a good musician and a fine cricketer. He was also very much a ladies' man. We stayed at an inexpensive boarding-house in Lower Rock Gardens for, I think, two pounds, five shillings per week including full board. At dinner he spotted two glamorous females and made good progress, and then we became involved in a rather mysterious episode which puzzles me to this day.

After a day or two of 'chatting-up', one of these girls said, 'A relation of ours has a nice bungalow at Peacehaven and has offered it to us for the weekend. Will you join us and spend the night?' Visions of all sorts of fun and games! We said, 'Yes', and told the landlady (our bedroom was actually in an annexe a street away so we had a different landlady from the girls, which is important to the story) that we were visiting relatives and would be out all night.

We met the girls at an agreed spot armed with tooth-brushes and, we hoped superfluous, pyjamas, and took a taxi to Peacehaven. I can still see that taximeter ticking away weeks of hard-earned savings while I wondered if the journey would ever end. At last we arrived and saw the bungalow was large and expensively furnished. I was ill at ease, as I could not equate this with our very simple boarding-house, which apparently was all the girls could afford. But—in for a penny...! After a few preliminary skirmishes the girls told us they were very sorry but they would have to go straight back as it was getting pretty late and *their* landlady had said if they stayed out all night she would feel obliged to write to their parents and inform them of the occurrence; but *we* could stay there and they would come out to us as early as possible the next day.

I was not happy at being there without some proof that we had had an invitation, so I asked them to leave the key, which they reluctantly did. Then the girls called for a taxi and left. This was something of an anti-climax and Charlie, who shared my discomfort at the set-up, absolutely refused to stay there any longer. 'What are we going to do?' I asked. 'Oh! walk back and go in for breakfast,' he replied. Of course, if we had had any sense we would have got back as quickly as possible and made some excuse for our return. However, we tied our pyjamas round our necks, as the night was chilly—and started to walk back. We spent the rest of the night in shelters on the front.

We entered the dining-room as usual for breakfast, but the girls seemed quite scared: 'What went wrong?' they asked, and just would not believe that nothing had. They immediately packed and went. Some days later I thought I saw them getting into a car with two coloured men. The whole thing remains a mystery to this day; but whatever it was, I think we were well out of it.

All my adult life I have taken at least one annual holiday. Going away from home to a change of air and scenery is necessary to 'recharge one's batteries'. Curiously enough I am certain one benefits not only from happy, comfortable holidays, but from poor ones too, unless one loses one's temper. Holidays, with the weather bad, the company depressing and the hotel third-rate, can nevertheless do you good. It is so nice to get back home and back to work to have a rest!

One such travesty of a holiday we had in Biarritz. I had expected sunshine, as in the South of France, but it can rain for long periods in the area around Biarritz and rain it did— incessantly for over a week. Many tourists in our hotel had not even brought a plastic mac, but we had and were able occasionally to walk for a few miles in the rain. Most of the party in the hotel were civil servants on an organised tour. At last the sun shone, so off we went for a swim. The waves were, I would say, twenty or thirty feet high and men were on look-out towers on the beach, ready to blow trumpets as a warning to bathers to get out if a huge and dangerous roller was on its way. The bathers, thus warned, would rush for the shore as if pursued by sharks. Added to this we all got covered with oil when sitting on the sands—incidentally this was my first experience of oil on a beach—and were badly bitten by sand-fleas. Children looked as if they had smallpox or some such disease but the fact was that the beach was 'alive' with these minute translucent creatures.

Being rather obviously at a loose end, we were kindly invited one evening to join up with the civil servants, who had organised an evening out. There was to be local dancing and what have you. The dancing was bad enough, but it was followed by an interminable recital from the French classics by a 'finished' French actress. This went on for an hour or two. Sitting on hard benches, too polite to leave, we waited and waited for an end which we felt would never come.

Walking back to the hotel one of the party remarked, 'ALL THE PLEASURES OF THIS HOLIDAY HAVE BEEN ABSOLUTE PURGATORY!' This wonderful summing up made me laugh, and I often quote it when holidays are unsatisfactory.

Time and time again, holiday adventures involve a measure of risk of one sort or another and this adds to the piquancy. Once in Killarney we took a trip and were informed we would start by jaunting-car to the lakes, where we would take a pony and return by boat. I do not know if anyone in the party realised that the pony ride was one of several miles, but since both my wife and I are quite good riders, this did not worry us. The short jaunting-car journey was uneventful and we gathered round the ponies and sorted things out. The reins, saddles and bridles were such that only Ireland could rustle up—tied with string, pieces missing, nothing matching. The distrust inspired by them was only exceeded by a glance at the 'ponies': all shapes and sizes, ungroomed, skinny ones, fat ones, tall ones, short ones, all looking as if they had just been rounded up—which, as it turned out, was pretty well what had happened.

Accidents on the way were surprisingly few. One woman had her hand crushed; a few people fell off, sustaining some shocks and bruising as the ponies bucked, shied or bolted. A woman ran behind us and twisted our ponies' tails to make them go faster and then said, 'You ride on, I will meet you at the end,' and disappeared, I assumed to take some short cut. I never saw her again. The scenery was magnificent, I am told, but we saw little of it, struggling as we were with our mounts. Afterwards I learned that my pony had never been ridden before, but usually pulled a buggy, and there was some uncertainty as to whether my wife's had ever done anything from birth but graze in the fields!

However, breathing sighs of relief at having reached our goal without personal mishaps, we now relaxed as we had only a pleasant boat trip ahead of us to take us back, traversing three lakes. The weather was good, after a week of very heavy rain, and the warm sunshine made a boat trip particularly enticing.

The whole party boarded an enormous rowing boat with four oarsmen and about fifteen passengers on board. We had traversed the first two lakes when I noticed that the boatmen seemed concerned about something: they argued and some changed places. As far as I could judge we were about to 'shoot the rapids'—another stunt dreamed up for the tourists, I thought!

Suddenly the boat gained momentum, and we shot along what appeared to be a channel between the high granite cliffs. One lake appeared to empty itself into the next through this funnel. Following the heavy rains there was an unusual amount of water and we were in the midst of a raging, boulder-strewn torrent. We were indeed 'shooting the rapids'! We passed under a bridge at the narrowest point, there was a bump, a lurch and a sound of splintering. I knew we had hit a rock and that a loaded boat like this would quickly sink.

Almost immediately there were cries from the stern as the water rushed through a hole in the bottom and the passengers were soaked as the water covered the seats. The boatmen skilfully manoeuvred the boat to a small island, and my wife always says that not only was I the first to jump ashore but the only one who did not get his feet wet! I have pointed out to her that it just so happened that I was fortunately placed and well up forward in the bow. The situation may have called for something heroic, but it was not forthcoming from me!

The boatmen proceeded to repair the hole, which was some six or seven inches in diameter. They did this mainly with old rags and strips of thin wood. We got back into the boat and in due course arrived back. I remarked to one of the boatmen that it surely was a close thing. After all, if we had capsized or sunk, we would have been caught in swirling rapids and even a good swimmer would have been very lucky if he had escaped being dashed against a rock. 'Sure,' he said, 'but don't say anything at the hotel as it makes things bad for the trade. You see, a boatload was drowned last week!' To this day I do not know if he was pulling my leg, but I never mentioned it. It could only happen in Ireland!

We went abroad each year and we were in Nice a few days before war was declared. We saw the mobilisation of the French Army. The staff of our small hotel appeared in their call-up uniforms. Our return journey was an experience and a most uncomfortable one, but the excitement of it all—for one still hoped that war would be averted—helped us to take it in good part and we thought we would get back sooner or later although trains were being cancelled and some tourists, fearful of being trapped if they delayed their departure, were abandoning their cars.

One unforgettable memory was of a Frenchwoman getting into our already overcrowded carriage on the train from Nice, followed by an impossible amount of luggage, which somehow willing hands squeezed into the corridor already jammed with people. She said philosophically, 'C'est la guerre.' My heart sank, for she seemed to accept it as inevitable.

During the war holidays abroad were, of course, out of the question but one of my staff, the senior assistant in Harrods library, had a cottage in Cornwall, which she frequently talked about. She had bought it 'furnished' for seventy-five pounds. I said that we would like to stay there, but she said it was far too primitive for me. There was, she said, only one room downstairs and upstairs was divided by thin match-boarding into two rooms. There was no running water, the lavatory was situated at the bottom of the garden, and we would have to live on sandwiches as there were no cooking facilities. We said we would still like to have it for a week or so, and there we had one of the most enjoyable holidays of our lives.

The cottage was one of a row of fishermen's cottages, delightfully situated, and there was a well of clear water shared by the cottagers. The people were so kind to us. Neighbours would leave flowers or fresh strawberries and raspberries and in no time I had 'organised' gourmet meals. There was a large fireplace which we needed at night; using timber washed up on the beach, we enjoyed the warmth it provided. There was a primus stove and I found, too, a tin oven.

I got all this working and the farmer let me have ducks, so we feasted on roast duck, fresh green peas, new potatoes, raspberries and dairy cream. It was all great fun, rather like camping out, as we prepared our meals and washed up on the wall in front of the cottage in the sunshine, where the Cornish air had a smell of its own, of flowers mingled with damp moss and cow-parsley.

The local fishermen took me out with them to collect their lobster pots. This was, I learned, something of a special privilege. When I met a local schoolmaster in the pub and told him I was going, he said that he wanted to come too, but they did not like him and would not take him. Before we returned, the fishermen 'hid' part of their catch in the last lobster pot. They did this when they had had a good day, as they did not want their rivals to know how well they were doing. They then sank the pot full of lobsters as a reserve to draw upon if the catch was poor.

One of the local publicans was something of an outcast, as he was 'living in sin'. No one was particularly concerned about the immorality, but jealous because the situation was financially convenient. The woman was a widow with a naval pension, which she would lose if she remarried. Wisely she decided to enjoy the best of both worlds. Who knows, both pension and bed-mate may have been all the sweeter to her because of the circumstances!

Truth is so often stranger than fiction, as I suppose most people have found from their own experiences. So often when I tell a true story, people are obviously sceptical. My wife and I were walking on Dartmoor and we set out to explore Wistman's Wood about which I had read in a guide-book. It is one of the curiosities of Dartmoor, near Two Bridges. The wood comprises groves of dwarf oak trees. They grow among the rocks on a boulder-strewn slope. On nearing the wood we were put off by firing from a nearby range, but with the aid of field-glasses, I thought I could see where they were firing from and common-sense suggested that they would not fire into the wood and damage it. So we continued and it was fortunate that we did so, for suddenly we were startled by a noise and there, trapped in a stone wall by its head, was a small black bullock. It had been there for a few days, as we could tell by the droppings, and its neck was sore and bleeding. It had put its head through a space in the wall and evidently reached down for some particularly succulent grass, trapping itself against a jutting stone. As there was no one in sight to help, I could only try to release it by putting my weight against the high stones on the wall and endeavouring to knock them down. After several efforts I succeeded in freeing the poor animal.

Now this is strange but true. The little bullock, overjoyed at its freedom, ran off about twenty feet then suddenly stopped, turned, looked at us and bellowed a 'thank you'! There was no other explanation, its 'thank you' was quite obvious. Then it dashed on to a stream, as of course it was parched. But it did not put the need to drink before the need to thank us.

It is a far cry from roughing it third-class across Europe in my youth to the luxury of holidays in the Bahamas and Bermuda in later years, made possible by comparatively in-pensive arranged tours. We had the most wonderful holiday experiences in Bermuda in 1968. The press had got hold of my being at Hatchards, the booksellers serving the Royal Household, and published the date of my arrival. The telephone rang and we were most kindly invited by Mr Kenneth Ives to 'make ourselves at home' in his lovely place on the island, called 'Heron's Nest'. The grounds go down to a secluded and superbly beautiful lagoon and my wife and I bathed and sunbathed in this 'paradise', with refreshments— some pretty potent!—being brought to us by members of Mr Ives's staff. He himself had returned to New York, but it was an extraordinarily kind gesture to extend to us this hospitality! It came about this way.

Mr Ives had called at Hatchards a year or two earlier and had said he was making arrangements on behalf of an American charity to furnish a library of books for the children of Antigua. The little native children had few books and he, representing the Mill Reef Fund, which is an American charitable organisation, wanted to buy for the library a really good, and large, selection of suitable books. I was naturally tremendously interested, as the supplying of books for children is very near to my heart. Once again holidays have helped me in my business, as it happened that the previous year I had been on holiday in the Caribbean, so I understood, and had more knowledge of executing, the order. Mr Ives was kind enough to say, when he telephoned us in Bermuda, that he was most appreciative of my efforts for the public library in Antigua and extended his hospitality to express his thanks. What a surprise! And just for doing my job!

Here, for a day or two, we felt like millionaires. There were live sea-horses where we swam—the first I had seen outside an aquarium. The bright sun illuminates to a considerable depth, and at night some hotels flood-light the water; so Bermuda is, among other things, a natural aquarium. But it is also a 'Garden of Eden'—or at least we thought it so. The people both black and white, the beautiful eyes of the black babies, the friendliness and cheerfulness, the glorious flowers, the beaches and the scenery, make this truly an

'Island Paradise'. Long may it remain so.

But the ability to enjoy simple holidays and the simple pleasures of life still remains, particularly to those of us not born with the proverbial silver spoon. A riverside pub, a crust of bread and cheese, a country lane, the smell of new-mown hay, the sight of a newly-born lamb, foal or calf, all these are things which are there to delight everyone, often giving more intense pleasure than the so-called luxuries of life.

People frequently say that they cannot afford a holiday, but why do they not go for a walking tour, or hire or borrow a bicycle? Good holidays need not necessarily be expensive. I always envy Stevenson and his *Travels with a Donkey*. I can think of nothing more delightful and exciting than to travel with light equipment for camping and the company of a donkey which would also take the load off one's shoulders. There are so many wonderful things to do and holiday pleasures are enhanced by the fact that they are a break from the routine of daily work. The pleasure would be dimmed if life were all one long holiday; that is one reason why retirement from business for a life of leisure so often proves disappointing.

I recall two contrasting fishing experiences, each with their excitement, the first in the quiet waters of the Thames and the second in the colourful, exotic setting of Bermuda.

My friend Charlie and I, with our respective wives, hired a cabin cruiser from Salters at Oxford and spent a week's holiday on the Thames, going as far as Windsor and back. We spent our days cruising, fishing and swimming and time passed very pleasantly; so much so, that we hardly ever used the radio we had taken with us. One evening I had left on my line a small dead dace and I simply threw the line into the water, laid the rod on top of the boat and thought no more about it. In the middle of the night I was awakened by a tapping noise. I first thought it must be a rat. Suddenly it came to me, it was my rod. I rushed out in pyjamas, grabbed the rod and reeled it in. I had caught a fine eel, well over two feet long. I held it in the air and shouted to the others who tumbled out of their bunks and gazed at it sleepily. But what to do with it? I was frightened to hold it—eels bite—and to put it down on the deck could end in chaos. There was I, in the dark, with a large eel dangling on my line. I did not know what to do and said so. Charlie kept saying, 'I do wish you hadn't caught the darned thing!" which, in the circumstances, wasn't very helpful.

At last I had a brainwave. I remembered seeing bowls of eels on fishmongers' slabs, so evidently they could not get out of a bowl. I got a bucket, to be on the safe side, cut the line and left the eel until morning. I then killed it, skinned it and cooked it. Jellied eels are regarded by many as a delicacy, but not by me!

But it was in Bermuda I had my most memorable and exciting fishing experience. The local bookseller, Ford Baxter, had arranged for me to accompany him and his friends on a fishing trip. We took a boat out into the blue water beyond the reef. The boat, fully equipped for deep-sea fishing, belonged to an extremely experienced coloured man who knew the waters and supervised the day's proceedings. All this was new to me.

Ford Baxter provided a large packet of frozen fry, which thawed out quickly in the hot sun. The boatman searched the waters for the fish we were after, sprinkling handfuls of the fry to attract them. Then with hand lines we fished with the fry for a fish they called round-robin, and in no time had twenty to thirty, each weighing three pounds or so. These fish, although fun in themselves to catch and regarded by many as good eating, were caught by us for bait for the large game fish. They were kept alive in a tank in the bottom of the boat.

Having caught enough, we started fishing in earnest and secured a number of quite large fish, one a king amber-jack, weighing seven to ten pounds and I caught my first shark, a small one of rather less than ten pounds. Then I was into something really big: after an hour's playing it I was exhausted and handed the rod over to the others to carry on. Ford fought the fish for another hour and a half and we had still not seen it. Ultimately I brought it to the surface. It was a big shark of between one and a half and two hundred-weight. Something of a disappointment as all on board would have preferred it to be a large game fish such as a marlin. At last it was alongside and the boatman hit it on the nose with a pole. That is the usual practice as it stuns the shark but it is no simple matter to hit it sufficiently strongly and in this instance the shark simply went mad, made a rush or two at the boat and then was off again to the bottom. The struggle went on for another half an hour or so and at last the shark was alongside, played out, but it was so big and dangerous to kill and bring aboard that we decided to let it go, so the boatman broke the line and the shark was 'back in business'.

But this was not the climax of the excitement, for just before we let the shark loose, there arose from the depths like an apparition, an enormous hammerhead shark. It was un-doubtedly waiting to attack the shark on our line, as fish sense when another is in trouble and wait the opportunity to seize it. Two or three times already that day we pulled a large fish aboard with little more than the head remaining. The whole fish was there right to the time of landing, yet a shark had snapped it in the last second.

This huge hammerhead shark, quite four times the size of the shark we had hooked, had been waiting. Altogether it was a thrilling and rather terrifying experience. It was an extraordinary sight to see this huge, mottled fish, almost the same colour as the sea, gradually appear near the surface.

Back on shore the boatman cleaned the fish we had caught, in the water by the landing stage, I first had a photograph of myself taken with the small shark I had caught earlier. My friends took a quantity of the nice fresh fish for eating, but somehow I had no appetite for fish that evening!

XVI

'What a nice name!' is a common reaction when a 'Joy' is introduced. Some go on to say that it is a name easily remembered—and sure enough the next time they meet me they call me 'Mr Love', a Freudian association of ideas.

At one time I used a quotation on my notepaper from Blake's poem 'Infant Joy'—which I like very much:

> I happy am,
> Joy is my name.

I could be excused this literary fancy, for at least it helped if people could not read my signature. A joke appeared in a college magazine where a man named Paine was on duty at night and my father was there during the day:

> "Paine" may endure for a night
> But Joy cometh in the morning.

The quotation is from the Book of Common Prayer, the name Paine being substituted for 'heaviness'.

A natural interest in the name has caused me to unearth the histories of a few Joys. They are little known, which is surprising, as they are colourful enough.

Joys have been in Oxford for at least two or three centuries and there are a number of tombstones in the nave of the church of St Mary the Virgin in Oxford High Street. I recall how impressed was Mr Bryant (managing director of Mowbray's, the religious booksellers, and a most distinguished Treasurer of the Booksellers Association), when he saw them, but the last time I visited the church, the pews had been moved and all the stones were covered. There is just one visible memorial tablet on a wall to 'Martha, wife of Thomas Joy'. Perhaps the departed Joys prefer resting beneath the pews to being walked on, for, as the following histories illustrate, the Joys have an intense love of liberty, a characteristic which is as strong today in me and all the Joys I have known.

Father confessed he knew little of the family's history but said the Joys had originally come from Ireland, and this is most certainly true, as the name Joy appears in very early Irish records. Following up this line of thought, I discussed the matter over the years with various people and ultimately was fortunate enough to find an Irish lady who said that the Joys were indeed Irish and that there was a book on the subject. I obtained this book and am largely indebted to it for the following brief account of the hero, Henry Joy, and his equally renowned sister, Mary Ann. The full story of a most interesting period of Irish history and of the remarkable Irish characters of the time is to be found in the book called *The Life and Times of Mary Ann McCracken* by Mary McNeill, published by Allen Figgis & Co. of Dublin.

The Joys were Calvinists and in all probability fled to England from religious persecution in France. Some went to Ireland with the armies of James I.

Francis Joy, the grandfather of Henry and Mary Ann, worked hard as a lawyer for the cause of Irish independence and to the end of his long life never spared himself in the service of his country. He was a great philanthropist and started the *Belfast News Letter* in 1733. This was the first newspaper to be printed in Belfast. He was also the first person in Ireland to bring any perfection to the process of printing.

The Mary Ann McCracken of the biography and her brother Henry I have mentioned were also descended from the Joys. She was a woman of great courage and compassion, with a mind of outstanding quality, but it is her brother, Henry Joy, who is the more romantic figure. Their family background obviously greatly influenced their lives.

Henry Joy was a handsome young man, with golden hair. Strongly actuated by the desire for social justice and the welfare of the poor, whose idol he became, he took part in the Antrim Revolt of 1798. He was a born leader of men, and rallied the men of Down, Antrim, Armagh and Tyrone and might well have succeeded in altering the course of Irish history, had not his plans been betrayed to General Nugent and his army defeated. Poverty, not Irish Nationalism in its later form, was the reason that led men like Henry Joy to risk their lives in a desperate struggle.

Henry Joy was captured but refused to betray his friends and for his leadership of the rebels was sentenced by court-martial (little more than a formality) and publicly hanged by the British. His brave sister, Mary Ann, whose life was deeply involved with that of her brother, visited him constantly during his imprisonment and she made repeated efforts to secure his release. Finally, she actually accompanied him to the place of execution and saw him hanged. She was sustained during this awful ordeal, curiously enough, by the hope of resuscitating his lifeless body when it came into her possession, by artificial respiration with the help of a doctor. She was keenly interested in medicine and was aware that this was sometimes possible, but as she later wrote, her 'golden-haired, handsome young brother was quite dead'. Mary Ann lived to a ripe old age and was not only a great reformer but also an early revivalist of Irish music and poetry.

When I visited Belfast as President of the Booksellers Association of Great Britain and Ireland, I found there was a Joy Street, commemorating Henry Joy. In my speech that evening I said, rather flippantly, that I felt to name a street in advance of my visit was more than one had a right to expect, even though the Irish were famous for their hospitality! But when I was told the true story regarding its name, I felt I could not compete with such heroism and should 'get the hell out' as quickly as possible.

I think it likely that the Oxford Joys left Ireland after the death of Henry. In my childhood, I recall seeing my great-grandmother and knew my grandmother over many years, but never knew a grandfather Joy. My father's father was, I believe, Manciple (bursar) at an Oxford college, possibly Christ Church. He died young, leaving a large family. And I think a Joy was once Vicar at Iffley, just outside Oxford. An interesting document came to light, well over one hundred years old, relating to the Oxford Gaol and signed by 'Thomas Joy (gentleman bailiff)'.

Many years ago a Mr Joy wrote to me from Philadelphia, saying he had written a book entitled, *The Joys of Philadelphia*, where many had been prominent citizens. Unfortunately he died before he could send me a copy of his book and I have been unable to procure one.

I fear the name may be dying out, as there seems to be a tendency for female predominance and survival. Joy sons often died in infancy or, like myself, lived in a family of sisters only. My father's brothers, too, had families mostly of girls.

Joy women show marked strength of character like Mary Ann McCracken and it is something of a family joke that, given a chance, they dominate their menfolk. Another splendid female Joy with all these characteristics lived in Victorian times. She was Mary Eliza Joy, later to become Mary Eliza Haweis.

Mary Eliza was the daughter of Thomas Musgrove Joy—a Victorian portrait painter of a great facility and skill, who began brilliantly enough and attracted the attention of Queen Victoria herself, though that patronage was short-lived. He had been greatly depressed by the death of his two sons at an early age, and possibly his work suffered. Thereafter he became somewhat embittered. He painted many famous people, including the popular heroine, Grace Darling, whose portrait brought him much fame, but his great interest was in 'subject' painting, and he laboured long at two mammoth canvasses, in the style of Frith's 'Derby Day', on Tattersalls— entitled 'The Yard' and 'The Ring'. However, though in a great measure a successful artist, he never attained an R.A. and this rankled.

Thomas Musgrove Joy's youngest daughter (Mary Eliza), married a popular preacher, Hugh Reginald Haweis, a love-match that developed certain incompatibilities as the years wore on, for he was extravagant, flirtatious and ambitious. Mary Eliza was economical and passionate but she, too, was ambitious. She possessed a flair for interior decoration and fashion design and showed great originality and energy of mind. Despite domestic difficulties she established a new standard of taste along Pre-Raphaelite lines, culminating in her masterpiece—the decoration of Rossetti's house in Chelsea. She was concerned with simplicity of effect and the use of inexpensive materials, as opposed to the claustrophobic ostentation of her day.

She won her point and became famous among the wealthy for her salons, her dresses and converted cottages, one of which she decorated entirely for fifty pounds, using rush-matting, colourful Japanese cotton rugs and what was, perhaps, the forerunner of non-iron, drip-dry material—curtains of Lowestoft fishing-net, because when 'washed and hung outside, this net dries by itself'.

She kept a journal, wrote several books on fashion and interior decoration and produced an edition of *Chaucer for Children*. She also wrote copious articles on every topic under the sun; partly to earn money for her son's education, but also because (as she once wrote to her husband), 'I shall go on doing well and looking well to the last, and I shall die in harness because I am so built.' A typical Joy!

Queen Victoria and Queen Marguerite of Italy both sent messages of sympathy to her family on her death, such was her influence, and I, too, salute the memory of this brave, enterprising woman who may well have been an ancestor of mine.

There is an excellent biography of Mary Eliza Haweis called *Arbiter of Elegance* by Bea Howe, published by the Harvill Press.

To end on a triumphal note, I tell the tale of Major Joy, who sounded the charge at the battle of Balaclava (the charge of the Light Brigade). Trumpet-Major Henry Joy was Staff-Trumpeter to Colonel the Earl of Lucan. He had many decorations: the Turkish Crimea Medal in 1855, the Crimea Medal in 1856, a medal for Distinguished Conduct in the Field, and the Long Service and Good Conduct medal.

The officers of the regiment desired to present Joy with a silver trumpet in exchange for the old one, but he preferred to use the trumpet that had made history and continued to blow his own. Trumpet-Major Henry Joy died 1893, and the officers of the 17th Lancers erected a memorial to him in Chiswick Parish churchyard, not far from where I live now. The trumpet is preserved with his medals and those of his son, Sergeant H. A. Joy—the latter include the Queen's South African Medal, the King's South African medal, and the Canadian War Service Badge—in the National Army Museum.

XVII

I feel I have never really left Oxford, for over the years I
have returned regularly, paying several visits during each
year to keep in touch with my sisters and numerous relatives
—for we are a clannish family. In the course of these visits I
frequently go over the ground of my boyhood adventures,
thinking back nostalgically.

For instance, if I start along the canal path from Hythe
Bridge Street, memories flood my mind. Here, a few hund-
dred yards along the canal, is the spot where I used to catch
river mussels. First I would look for a crack in the mud at
the bottom of the canal, which at the side is only a foot or so
deep. Then slowly pushing through the water a long grass
stem, I would deftly insert it into the crack, which was in fact
the slightly open mussel buried in the mud, only this slight
opening indicating its presence. One had to be accurate first
time. If one was successful, the mussel immediately closed
tightly and one could pull it slowly to the surface. If one
missed, the mussel would feel the touch and close up giving
no further chance. I was optimistic enough to believe that one
day I might find a pearl in one.

As one proceeds along the canal path, there is the narrow
lock for barges and over the bridge towards the railway line a
large turntable for the goods engines. Under the very low
bridge one comes to Tumbling Bay, to which we walked early
in the mornings, with the mist rising off the river, to bathe.
Tumbling Bay is one of Oxford's bathing places. It branches

off from the main river and when we were children it was particularly exciting, as all bathers had to be ferried over. On reaching the other side, the females went into their high-fenced bathing place and the males walked on to their separate one.

Girls, my sisters tell me, could borrow what were called bathing costumes. These were blue cotton garments, usually faded and coming well below the knee, as the attendant was not discerning regarding sizes and often issued costumes much too large for the borrower. In those less affluent days it was quite customary for bathers to borrow costumes; few children possessed them. Continuing along the towpath, past Tumbling Bay towards Medley, is the spot where my friend Charlie caught a pike weighing over ten pounds, which later was proudly displayed on a fishmonger's slab in George Street. Trying for another in the same spot with characteristic optimism, to my surprise I caught two pike of about three to four pounds each and lost a third, from which I learned that two or three males, often smaller than the female, are likely to be in attendance.

So on to what was once Medley Weir, where from Bossoms' large floating boathouses I at times hired a rowing boat for sixpence. This charge was made for one person. I do not know if the boats were not safe to hold more but once out of sight we picked up a friend or two. Occasionally we would be caught doing this and the boat would be taken from us.

In dwelling on the events of one's life to a far greater degree than usual—as is necessary when writing autobiography—the awareness of the passage of time and the short span of man's life is uppermost in one's thoughts.

One has to try to get all sorts of things in perspective. Sir Basil Blackwell was kind enough to say to me recently that he and colleagues at Oxford admired and were fond of me because, with all my success, I had not changed, and others have been kind enough to say much the same thing. This is most pleasing if true, and I hope it is true. Yet, if true, there is little virtue in it, for like most people, I am sure, I am not very conscious of having been successful. Any success is tempered in my mind with opportunities lost and an awareness of my human failings and limitations and of other people's greater successes.

I admit to an enormous feeling of gratitude for the advantage of a comparatively humble start which, I am certain, sharpened my wits, for a sound education, and for all the advantages of Oxford life, so much of which I have, until recently, taken for granted. Just the other day, when I was reminiscing with a friend born in a country cottage well outside Oxford, he told me how impressed he had been by the high standard in our house, by our well-laid table, our general behaviour and deportment compared with their country ways, made necessary for larger families as there was no room in a country cottage to sit at table: children took a helping from the bowl of stew and curled up to eat it in a corner on the floor.

I am particularly grateful for the blessings the book trade has brought me and especially for having thereby met many of the most interesting people of my generation. Yet I cannot be smug, for I question how far I really used any of my talents to the full. I feel I have often been very lazy and it was reluctance to continue studying more than anything else which led me into bookselling. Perhaps I should have studied for a degree. The present generation may find it curious that I am grateful for having been forced to study certain things against which I mentally fought at the time, since I benefited in after years. Medicine does not taste nice but it does you good.

I conclude that a happy life is, in itself, a successful life; and that happiness is found in the art of living. Happiness if pursued can be elusive. Men—I believe most men—find a lot of satisfaction and happiness in their work. Those who regard work as drudgery cannot understand how it is that many people, including top executives who obviously from birth have been so placed financially that they did not have to earn a living, want to work. I feel grateful for having had the necessity to earn a living, as it brings with it a disciplined self and develops latent possibilities.

I feel, too, that my generation has been especially fortunate, as we experienced all that was good and bad in the old order and benefited from much of the new. We saw country roads empty excepting for an occasional horse and cart; we knew England with a smaller population, so queues were unknown —the word was not even in common parlance until the 1914-1918 war. We enjoyed food with all its natural flavour, unpolluted rivers in which we could swim and enjoy the crystal clear water. We saw the invention or the development of the motor car, the aeroplane, cinema, radio, television and we have benefited from the advances in medical science; and the impact of all these things we can relate to a way of life before they existed.

I love travelling abroad but always look forward to returning home, for England is a very good home and the more one travels the more one appreciates this.

Seeing the dolly birds of today, we wish we were young again—how young I wonder? I recall my father saying quite seriously when he was eighty-five years old, 'I wish I was ten years younger!' Some people tell me they would not wish to be young again, as they despise much of the change which has taken place; but surely youth is a most wonderful thing in itself, which passes all too soon! To have a young, healthy body is the greatest gift of all.

Change is not necessarily improvement but, during my lifetime, things have improved almost beyond belief. One saw poverty, and all too often with it a loss of self-respect. It was no uncommon sight to see women wearing their husbands' old peak caps on their heads in the poorer districts of Oxford. That could hardly have assisted morale. So much of the misery of 'the good old days' has been greatly alleviated. My mother and father would say from time to time that they were 'born too soon' because they could see the advantages youth would enjoy. I, in my turn, feel the same today. It is a wonderful age, full of promise, and it is impertinent to think that the present generation will fail to make good use of it. In the course of my work I interview young people daily and overall one cannot help being impressed by their charm, ability and responsible attitude, so different from the conception which might be gained from certain sections of the press and TV.

Of course, I have been lucky and no one would deny that one needs a measure of luck in life. Even good health or beauty are gifts from the gods—or, if you like, just luck. Yet I have met many quite famous people who have succeeded in spite of enormous handicaps, their determination and patience having ultimately brought them to the desired goal.

To succeed, it is necessary to take chances, and I am sure it is better to live adventurously or, at times, even dangerously than to have security with boredom. Looking back, I think I should have been more adventurous—just for the fun of it—although it would not necessarily have helped in my career and might well have jeopardised it. Another lesson that I have learned is not to worry. Hardly any of the things which caused concern at the time, actually happened, and in any case worrying would not have helped in any way, indeed the reverse, since worry can create the very thing you fear.

Having spent over fifty years in business, I have some measure of regret that my life was not devoted to work of greater value to mankind, such as medical research or the practice of medicine, but I hope that through these pages I have conveyed that bookselling is a career not without value —as, indeed, is retailing generally. I hope, too, that I have made the point that management makes a contribution and it is a privilege which carries with it the responsibility for the welfare of the staff. If one has succeeded in doing a good job in these fields one has not lived in vain.

It is nice to have enjoyed many of the more luxurious things of life, particularly in later years, made so much sweeter by the very fact that one has not always been used to them. It is gratifying to go to the top in one's trade or profession. Luck, as I have said, may help you to get there, but only hard work and ability will keep you there. When people express their gratitude for some help one gave them somewhere along the road, it is, in itself, a reward, but at the same time one wonders how many times one has failed.

When I left some of my posts, those who had worked with me said afterwards that the fun had gone and the job was now boring. This I treasure as a compliment because personal enthusiasm makes work more fun, not only for oneself but for others. Nothing is more infectious. Perhaps I have never quite grown up!

Whatever the struggle and set-backs, and naturally I have had my share of them, my life in Oxford, the book trade, the departmental store world has been *Mostly Joy*.

I learned a poem from a man I met whilst on holiday—he was aged over eighty and *on his honeymoon*. I liked it so much that I memorised it. I now put it down from memory as I cannot trace it in any book of poems accessible to me. I find a reference, however, attributing it to Edward Tuck and N. S. Fritsch. I hope I may be forgiven any inaccuracy and I hope, too, that it will mean as much to some of my readers as it has meant to me.

> Age is a quality of mind
> If you have left your dreams behind.
> If hope is cold,
> If you no longer look ahead,
> If your ambition's fires are dead,
> Then you are old.
>
> But if in life you seek the best,
> And if for life you have a zest,
> If love you hold
> No matter how the years go by,
> No matter how the birthdays fly,
> You are not old.

APPENDIX

Presidential Address
delivered by the author at the
Booksellers Conference at
Folkestone, May 1958

I bid you all welcome to this conference and to the 63rd annual general meeting. I hoped that by holding it at Folkestone it would make it possible both from a geographical and an economic angle for a record number to be present.

Our booksellers' conference is many things, but first in importance, surely, is the getting together of the family of booksellers, to discuss business matters certainly, but, more importantly perhaps, to gain by the exchange of ideas and by getting to know one another outside the conference room. Our conference, it has been said, can be divided into happy ones and historic ones, and I hope that this may prove to be both. In spite of many difficulties facing booksellers ours is a happy trade.

Over the years many difficulties have been solved by the fact that officers and members have known from personal contacts, often made at these conferences, their publisher counterparts, and my presidential year has been no exception. I have used personal contacts to full advantage, and I hope from them that I may have accomplished more than appears on the surface at this date.

I would remind you of the subjects covered by my predecessor, Mr Donne-Smith, in his presidential address last year. He drew attention to matters which he said were significant rather than merely striking. He recalled that at the previous conference at Thurlestone he had said that the net book system was in danger of disintegration. He dealt with partial remaindering, particularly in the form of a certain new book club, and with the School Libraries Licence, when he reported that the Booksellers Association had contracted out. He said 'the old trade recognition system had suffered almost to the point of extinction'.

Age-old Problems

From Mr Donne-Smith's remarks of last year I would go back a century and by quoting just a few extracts from the invaluable *One Hundred Years* recently published by *The Bookseller* it will be seen that the problems of today are much as they have been in the past.

' "Mr. Gladstone says that English books are abominably dear, and so they are", *The Bookseller*, March, 1860.'

'By an advertisement in this month's *Bookseller*, it will be seen that a considerable number of the trade are turning their attention from books to sewing machines, by which they get a good profit, on which there is no silly and uncalled-for discount, and which the proprietors will not allow to be undersold. The Wanzer Company protect the interests of retailers in a manner which might be imitated by publishers.'—*March*, 1866.

'It appears to be very generally conceded that the booksellers of the present day are, as a whole, deficient in that precise knowledge of books and authors possessed by many of the older members of the trade. Many reasons can be given for this deficiency; one, and perhaps the chief, being the number of new authors and the variety of new editions of every form and price.' —*January*, 1870.

'Sir,—We are convinced that if publishers and booksellers could meet more often on neutral ground, and in good fellowship and free debate, we should all benefit by it.'—*June*, 1934.

It will not therefore surprise you that during my presidential year I have been concerned with such age-old problems as the improvement of terms and conditions of supply, and above all the safeguarding of the Net Book System.

Approach to Publishers

Dealing with the first, my approach has been perhaps rather different from my predecessor's. I have not dealt so much with the Publishers Association in matters of terms— because, as you know, that Association cannot make commitments on behalf of its members involving terms—but with individual publishers and small groups; and I have asked them to examine the position realistically and see how far we are in agreement, and if change is necessary, how we can work towards such change. It must cause concern to publishers that bookshops are obviously going out of business or altering their methods of trading to a degree that makes books relatively unimportant to the businesses. You will have noted that the Publishers Association stated in its annual report that 'when the terms of the Net Book Agreement were brought to the notice of the booksellers, in a rather startling number of cases the reply was "no longer selling books"'. We sorely need statistics and had I had a further period in office I would have requested the setting up of our own statistical department similar to that of the Retail Distributors' Association. Such figures are badly needed.

Attitude to Net Book Agreement

Turning to the net book system, whilst it is true that the Net Book Agreement, 1957, was registered by the Publishers Association under the Restrictive Trades Practices Act, it is also true that, through ignorance in some quarters, personal ends, or particular forms of publishing, it is still in some danger. This Association was formed to support the Net Book Agreement and there is no uncertainty in our attitude towards it. The system is, we believe, in the interests not only of the trade as a whole but important to the cultural life of the community. Without such a system there could be few if any good bookshops. The Net Book Agreement has over the years proved itself. It is regarded by many in high places as an ideal; an agreement which, although in some measure a restrictive practice, is by no means a monopoly and works to the benefit of the people as a whole.

In view of this it has been difficult for booksellers to understand why the Publishers Association appears to shrink whenever any questions are asked regarding the Agreement, rather than to say, 'Well, here is the whole thing, we are proud of it and that is that'. In fairness I am assured in my consultations with Mr. Parsons, the president of the Publishers Association, that their policy is based on the preservation of the net book system, although the two associations may not altogether see eye to eye on the best methods of securing this object. Any tampering or weakening of the system, in the opinion of many in the trade, may prove disastrous, and I must say that I am very deeply concerned with the policy of the Publishers Association which appears so much at variance with ours. The question I ask is, how far can the net book system be preserved in a 'free for all'?

'Free-for-all'

The J.A.C. prevents no one from opening in opposition, but works to secure some standard in bookselling and as far as possible some quality in personnel; and to ensure that the net book system be observed. A 'free-for-all' could only end in there being no trade for anyone. If the net book system is weakened it will severely damage our export trade because that is sustained only by a healthy home trade. I had the pleasure of visiting Holland early in my presidential year and it appeared to me that they had managed things better there, and I invited their president (Mr H. W. Blok) to attend our conference and he will tell of the Dutch bookselling methods from which I think we may learn a lot.

How long will it be before publishers are looking for outlets for their books? Can this be what Mr Victor Gollancz meant, who is quoted as having said recently, 'Publishing is indeed on its last legs. It may last my lifetime but not much more.' I am convinced that there is a future, indeed a great future, for both bookselling and publishing, but it rests not only on goodwill between the two but upon careful examination of the trade problems by the associations.

Regular Meetings

This is one of the last important speeches I shall make to you and I conclude by appealing to you all and all publishers to do everything in your power to bring about regular quarterly meetings of the officers of the two associations. Without such close working not only will there be misunderstanding but there will be lack of progress. Some progress in this direction has already been made. A joint meeting is to be called and every effort was made to call one before this conference but that was not found to be possible at short notice. The president of the Publishers Association did, however, specially call to see me to explain the attitude of the P.A. to School Library Discount and the J.A.C., and in spite of any differences of opinion I would say that Mr Parsons and Mr Sanders have been kindness itself to me and we have never had a cross word. The P.A. persists in its policy but is nevertheless anxious and careful to avoid friction.

'Summit Talks' Necessary

This is a time which is revolutionary rather than evolutionary; it is, as I see it, only by the right action today that we jointly have a bright future. We must discount the diehards, those old friends who say glibly that 'if you give them $33\frac{1}{3}$ per cent they will soon ask for 40 per cent' or 'postpone the issue until they forget all about it'. Many publishers realise with booksellers that if such counsels prevail we are all sunk. Our object should be to discover what terms and trading conditions are required for mutual prosperity. Your new 'Terms, Trade Practices and Carriage Committee' has much to do, but 'summit talks' covering a wide field are necessary. It is no longer sufficient for the two presidents just to meet occasionally over the luncheon table, events move quickly and the problems are grave. This bookselling which we all hold dear means much more to us than our bread and butter; indeed, throughout the ages booksellers have been prepared to make tremendous sacrifices.

The Greatest Possession We Have

I end with a phrase from the text of *My Fair Lady* which I find inspiring: 'Think what we are dealing with, the majesty and grandeur of the English language. It is the greatest possession we have. The noblest sentiments that ever flowed in the hearts of men are contained in its extraordinary, imaginative and musical mixture of sounds.'

The future is in your hands—and may this conference illumine a small flame to lighten the way.